Einstein
and the
Image of God

A Response to Contemporary Atheism

by

Richard W. Kropf

Einstein and the Image of God

Copyright © 2015 by Richard W Kropf

All rights reserved. No part of this book
may be reproduced or transmitted in any form
or by any means, electronic or mechanical,
including photocopying, recording, or by
information storage and retrieval system,
without permission of the author.

Kropf, Richard W., 1932-

    224 pp., includes bibliography, index

IBSN-13: 978-1514879320
IBSN-10: 1514879328

Initial Publication date: August 1915
Subsequent revisions: October 2015, July 2016

Stellamar Publications
PO Box 315
Johannesburg, MI 49751-0315

Cover: "Christ Enthroned"
A contemporary icon inspired by the work
of Andre Rublev (c. 1410).
Permission of Madonna House Apostolate
Combermere, Ontario

Dedicated to all God-seekers.

Contents

Acknowledgments — vii
Preface by Anthony J. Morse — ix
Introduction by the Author: — 1

Part I: The Unknown God — 13

Chapter 1: Atheism and the God of Experience — 15
    A: Freud and the Father Figure as God — 16
    B: America's Four Gods — 19
    C: Varieties of Religious Experience — 24
    D: Personhood: Can It Apply to God? — 27
    Conclusion to Chapter 1 — 30

Chapter 2: Science and the God of Reason — 33
    A: Being and Existence — 36
    B: Design Revisited — 40
    C: God and the Problem of Evil — 45
    Conclusion to Chapter 2 — 50

Chapter 3: The New Deism — 55
    A: God In Spinoza's Thought — 58
    B: Reality in Process — 63
    C: A Non-theistic Christianity? — 67
    Conclusion to Chapter 3 — 70

Part II: Christ the Image of God — 75

Chapter 4: The Historical Jesus — 77
    A: Did Jesus Exist? — 77
    B: Levels of Tradition — 80
    C: The Miracle Stories — 84
    D: The Question of the Kingdom — 87
    E: The Death of Jesus and Its Aftermath — 94

Conclusion to Chapter 4   99

Chapter 5: The Christ of Christian Tradition   103
   A: The Historical Question Revisited   104
   B: From Paul to John   105
   C: From Antioch to Alexandria   110
   D: Constantine's Intervention   114
   E: The Chalcedonian Compromise   118
   Conclusion to Chapter 5   119

Chapter 6: The Christ of the Future   125
   A: God within Process   127
   B: Teilhard and the Cosmic Christ   131
   C: Cosmological Reconsiderations   140
   Conclusion to Chapter 6   143

Part III: Christ and the God beyond God   147

Chapter 7: Christ and the God beyond Images   149
   A: Rethinking Christology   150
   B: Christ and the Triune God   156
   C: The God beyond God   159
   D: Hope and Faith beyond Beliefs   164

Some Concluding Afterthoughts   173

Bibliography   181

Index   193

About Author   207

Acknowledgments

First and foremost, thanks are due to Anthony J. Morse, especially for his part in urging me to finally write this book, and whom I must also thank for his gracious Preface. "Tony" and I have been good friends for more than a quarter of a century and his extensive explorations into literature and philosophy — including the many books he has loaned or on some occasions even bought for me to read — have been an often unrelenting challenge for me to ponder as a theologian.

Next, I must thank Patrick Stonehouse, a fellow stargazer (and much more keen-eyed than I, Patrick having discovered a hitherto undiscovered comet in 1989 — not long after he and I first met). He was the first to urge me to explore Einstein's life and thought, and has graciously served as the science adviser in this book's writing, both correcting some of my otherwise vague grasp of more technical matters as well as calling attention to some of the latest discoveries that may have otherwise escaped my notice.

Thanks also to Rudi Edel, who both urged me to hold and helped me organize a weekend workshop back in June of 2014, on the subject that constitutes the first part of this book, and to Karen Gritter for her theological insights and to all the others who attended and who collectively helped this book become more focused on the problem that people have in relating to God as a "person", rather than being lost in the abstractions of philosophy. Thanks also to my old friend and neighbor, Richard Bruot, and to Maureen Derenzy, head librarian at Otsego County Library, and Jackie Skinner of the library staff and Colleen McIntyre Wisniewski, for their help in choosing a title and formatting the book's cover, and to another old friend, Harold Wessell, for his editorial assistance.

Einstein and the Image of God

All the biblical quotations are from the New Revised Standard Version of the Bible published by Harper Books, unless otherwise noted.

Special thanks are due to Princeton University Press for having made available to the public Alice Calaprice's *The Ultimate Quotable Einstein,* as well as Max Jammer's study of *Einstein and Religion,* both of which have proved to be a real goldmine regarding Einstein's views regarding God and religion.

Thanks to Wipf & Stock Publishers for the permission to quote extensive passages from John B. Cobb's anthology *Religions in the Making.*

Although I have tried to refrain from any extensive quotations from the writings of Pierre Teilhard de Chardin, I must thank Harcourt Brace Jovanovich, HarperCollins, Harper & Row, and William Collins and Sons for their dedication to making Teilhard's works available to the English speaking public, as well as to the *Fondation Teilhard de Chardin* in Paris and the Paris Province of the Society of Jesus for making available to me so much of Teilhard's still unpublished writings.

I also wish to congratulate David Ray Griffin and Donald W. Sherburne and The Free Press/Simon & Schuster of New York for their corrected 1978 edition of A. N. Whitehead's *Process and Reality* which nevertheless preserved the pagination of the earlier Harper Torchbook edition which I had been using.

Finally, my thanks to all the other writers and publishers whose works I have cited, and especially to the Amazon Corporation for making so many out-of-print, hard-to-find and/or public domain books available, many of them in electronic form, some even for free, to the public.

Preface
by Anthony J. Morse

As a foreword or preface to this book, the author, Richard Kropf, who has been one of my closest friends over the past thirty or so years, asked me to compose a survey of readings that we have shared leading up and through "The New Atheism" movement that is one of the subjects of this new book. In fact, I had loaned him most of these books — or even bought a few extra copies just for him to read and have handy for reference, since he lives in a rather isolated area in the woods of Northern Michigan.

But first let me make explicit my own position. As I have already stated and written in the past about God, in the face of this mysterious unknown, agnosticism is the proper stance. With an acclaimed revelation though one must study and seek the best explanation, and short of dogmatism — judge! Agnosticism in this case leads to relativism, little dialogue, and less thinking. Or again, as Nietzsche said: "To judge is the nut of existence." It contests the biblical "Judge not, that ye be not judged." Thus, of late, I have, like Albert Einstein, adopted Spinoza's God.

However, my dialogue with Kropf on this whole subject began some years before the so-called "New Atheism" and the "New Atheists" burst upon the scene. It began when I first loaned Kropf my copy of the philosopher Walter Kaufmann's 1950 study *Nietzsche: Philosopher, Psychologist, and Anti-Christ*. This book made Kaufmann famous, for he more than anyone else made intellectuals shed their misconceptions about Nietzsche and recognized him as one of the most important thinkers in Western philosophy and one of the greatest writers in German literature. But this was not the case in 1947 when Kaufmann arrived at Princeton University.

Einstein and the Image of God

He was introduced to Albert Einstein — who questioned him about the thesis on which he was working. Upon hearing Kaufmann, the shocked Einstein responded: "But that is simply dreadful!" So it seems that Kaufmann had his work cut out for himself. I also at first loaned Kropf my copy of Kaufmann's own philosophical outlook that so impressed me after I attended Kaufmann's lectures as a visiting professor of philosophy at the University of Michigan when I was a student there.

The other misconception about Nietzsche was the failure of the public knowing the total context of Nietzsche's claim that "God is dead". "God is dead. God remains dead...And we have killed him. How shall we comfort ourselves, the murderers of all murderers?" ("The Gay Science" sec: 125, translated by Walter Kaufmann, *The Portable Nietzsche*). In this same vein of blame, Kaufmann coined the word "empiricide" (think "suicide") seeing science and rationality of man as responsible for God's death! Ten years after my graduation I attended another lecture by Kaufmann at the University of Michigan and talked to him briefly afterwards. He died all too soon ten years later, in 1980, at the age of 59.

As for the "New Atheists" themselves, Christopher Hitchens was an Oxford-educated English journalist and critic whose books I had read before hearing him on stage at the Apollo Theater in London, 2002. This was a full five years before his 2007 international best seller *God Is Not Great: How Religion Poisons Everything*. The phrase "New Atheism" had not been coined, but Hitchens was a very colorful and controversial character, even then. I was not familiar with his anti-religious stance so I was surprised to hear him say "The axis of evil is Judaism, Christianity, and Islam!" In a short chat with Hitchens in the Apollo Lounge afterwards, I asked

Preface

him if I had heard correctly. "Yes" he answered. We talked about some of his books — one of which I had just read, *Letters to a Young Contrarian*" (2001). He said that this book was better than the one being promoted that evening! I was getting the tone of his polemic and a first-hand preview of "The New Atheism".

Subsequently, Sam Harris's best seller, *The End of Faith*, won the 2005 PEN Award for Nonfiction and is published in more than fifteen languages. He has a degree in philosophy from Stanford University and a Ph.D in neuroscience from UCLA, and to all appearances at the time, seemed to be an unwavering materialist, and hence, atheist. So I was surprised to read in his new 2014 book, *Waking Up: A Guide to Spirituality Without Religion*, about how much time Harris has spent on meditation and Buddhism. His scientific approach produces a most convincing picture. Harris says that religion is especially rife with bad ideas, calling it "one of the most perverse misuses of intelligence we have devised."

Richard Dawkins is an evolutionary biologist and English ethnologist at Cambridge. His 2006 book *The God Delusion*, capitalizing on his popular and controversial *The Selfish Gene* (1975) started to solidify the "New Atheist" movement. In his newer book Dawkins contends that a supernatural creator almost certainly does not exist and that religious faith is a delusion — "a fixed false belief."

Daniel Dennett is the only professional philosopher of the group that Hitchens dubbed "The Four Horsemen of the New Atheism." Dennett has a "D.Phil" from Oxford and a teaching post at Tufts University. While Kropf and I have shared our impressions of Dennett's 1995 *Darwin's Dangerous Idea*, and his 2006 *Breaking The Spell: Religion as a Natural Phenomenon*, Kropf remains convinced that while Dennett is a good philosopher of science, Dennett's avoidance of ontology

Einstein and the Image of God

or the central question addressed by Krause (why there is something rather than nothing) is all too obvious.

However, as Kropf notes, there had been, all along until his death in 2014, a fifth aspirant to that exclusive group, one whose efforts in that direction had long predated the other four. This was Victor J. Stenger, a long-time professor of physics at the University of Hawaii, capped with an emeritus post as Professor of Philosophy at the University of Colorado. His dozen or so books, the first dating back to the late 1980s, and most of them dealing with the universe and its origins, are all more or less explicitly atheistic in outlook, culminating with his 2012 *God and The Folly of Faith: The Incompatibility of Science and Religion.* In it he continued to be a strong advocate for removing the influence of religion from scientific research, commercial activity, and the political process, and he coined the popular phrase "Science flies you to the moon. Religion flies you into buildings." But Kropf also notes that Stenger, unlike "the four horsemen", seems to have understood not only the full breadth of the scientific, and especially cosmological, and ultimately ontological issues — as well as (having been raised a Catholic) having some respect for the theologians who wrestled with these issues in past ages and continue to do so.

Last on this list of books of note which seem to be dedicated to aggressively promoting atheism, we have Lawrence Krauss' 2012 best-selling *A Universe from Nothing: Why There is Something Rather than Nothing.* Krauss specializes as a professor of theoretical physics and cosmology at MIT. Krauss states that the premise that something cannot come from nothing is often used as an argument for the existence of an uncaused cause, or creator. But in a dazzling display of double-talk he affirms that the laws of physics allow for the universe to be created from a quantum vacuum, or to his

Preface

mind "nothing", but, then, finally admits (in Chapter 9), that in this case, "Nothing Is Something."

Thus ends the brief survey of atheistic books that Kropf and I have studied and discussed over the last ten or so years. There are many more books on atheism, some good, some bad. For a fuller survey of the subject, one should consult Peter Watson's 2014 *The age of Atheism: How We Have Sought to Live Since the Death of God*. I would also add to this list of books we have shared one more: it is Antonio Damasio's *Looking for Spinoza*. Although written by a neuroscientist on the subjects of "joy, sorrow and the feeling brain," it underlines Spinoza's rejection of Descartes' dualistic view of human nature, one of the features that especially attracted Einstein to Spinoza's philosophy ("What Life Means to Einstein", 1929: Calaprice, 152).

So where does all this leave "The "New Atheism" and "The New Atheist" and how is Kropf going to deal with them? As I see it, when it comes to thinking about other religions other than the one in which we were raised, we are all atheists! So is it really God we are talking about? When you read the "New Atheists" you see that they are, really not so much reacting to arguments in favor of there being a God, but rather more to various and different aspects of the human predicament — war, poverty, disease, suffering, nature, the cosmos etc. — that to their minds indicate that there isn't one. Can we really know for certain the beginning (cause), the purpose (plan), the end (eternity) of life? Hitchens preferred to be called anti-theist than an atheist — as does Lawrence Krauss. And in their angry outbursts are mostly talking about certain people and events and the ideas that produced them or were produced by them, but not God. Sam Harris, being a neuroscientist, speaks of the mind that is physically only the brain, part of our body. Thus, to Harris there is no soul and

Einstein and the Image of God

therefore (however illogically argued from that) no God either. Dawkins advocates evolutionary processes, all physical, all observable and with no evidence of God. Dennett and Stenger talk of suns with beginnings and ends, and of planets with beginnings and ends — but no God. And so we end all the above with the materialistic position, not so much of atheism but agnosticism.

Conversely, the Abrahamic religions (Judaism, Christianity, Islam) rely for their foundations on the various revealed "truths" that have come to them through holy persons, divinely caused events, sacred scripture, etc., no matter how much philosophy the theologians have used to try to make sense of it all. In this new book Kropf will wend his way through these various paths to counter particularly the more negative agnosticism and atheisms currently afoot. Therefore I will end this preface by taking a look at two thinkers Kropf feels supply some answers to this important discussion: Philosopher Baruch Spinoza and scientist Albert Einstein. Let us hear from Spinoza first:

> Nature does not work with an end in view. For the eternal and infinite Being which we call God or Nature, acts by the same necessity as that whereby it exists... Therefore, as he does not exist for the sake of an end, so neither does he act for the sake of an end; of his existence and his action there is neither origin nor end" (*Ethics*, Preface to Part V).

Is this monism, materialism, pantheism, naturalism, determinism, theism, or even atheism? Nevertheless, Einstein said that he believed in Spinoza's God. According to Einstein, this belief led to a religious feeling that he described as taking

Preface

... the form of a rapturous amazement at the harmony of natural law, which reveals an intelligence of such superiority that, compared with it, all the systematic thinking and acting of human beings is an utterly insignificant reflection... Hence it is precisely among the heretics of every age that we find men who were filled with the highest kind of religious feeling and were in many cases regarded by their contemporaries as atheist, sometimes also saints. Looked at in this light, men like Democritus, Francis of Assisi, and Spinoza are closely akin to one another. (Einstein, *The World As I See It*. 1934: Calaprice, 333.)

However, as Kropf will show, quite convincingly, what Einstein may have been trying to express but lacked was the radically evolutionary recasting of Spinoza's insights in the "process" thought of Alfred North Whitehead, which Kropf supplements with a more explicitly Christian interpretation of evolution as envisioned by the Jesuit paleontologist Pierre Teilhard de Chardin.

In the ending of his book, Kropf creates a synthesis that is not a collection of dogmas, doctrines, or creeds, but a sublime sort of thinking that rises above the various certainties usually offered by academic theologians. This thinking celebrates the greatness and goodness of our mysterious and marvelous created being. At the end, you have a philosopher and a theologian who expertly guides us between the stubborn rocks of religious tradition and the shifting shoals of contemporary science.

Anthony Jenckes Morse, April, 2015

Einstein and the Image of God

Introduction
by the Author

This book is about the largely unknown and invisible God and the man, Jesus of Nazareth, who Christians believe was sent by God to be his replica or image. But, let's face it: especially today, in the wake of the mayhem of September 11, 2001 and all the atrocities that have followed it, the whole idea of religion in general, and the image of God in particular, have suffered. As a result, perhaps no subject of debate today draws more heat — and confusion — than the topic of belief in God and its opposite, atheism, especially the so-called "New Atheism" that has garnered so much publicity and growing popularity since that tragic event. This book has been especially written, first of all, for those whose belief in God has been shaken by all this controversy, as well as for those unbelievers who are open-minded enough to seriously consider – or to possibly reconsider if they have already have been swayed by the recent onslaught. As this book will make clear from the start, a major part of the problem is a great amount of confusion as to just what is meant by the word "God", with a multitude of distorted notions originating on both sides of the debate.

However, at the same time, this book was also written for those Christians whose beliefs about Jesus have been challenged by the avalanche of New Testament scholarship — most of it serious, but some of it sensationalist — that began well over a century ago but has only increased over more recent years. In the face of all this, the question has to be asked: can Christian beliefs about the divinity of Jesus be any longer sustained?

Einstein and the Image of God

Thus, any potential reader should be forewarned. This book is not for everyone. Although it has been written for the educated layperson who has not been especially trained in philosophy or theology, it will prove rather demanding in that the reader will be dragged, perhaps somewhat reluctantly, into having to grapple with some key concepts in those fields. Moreover, in terms of personal maturity, the reader needs to have progressed far enough to have begun to understand, or at least sense within one's own self, the difference between faith and the various beliefs that express that faith. As we will soon see, while this difference has long been implicit in the teaching of the spiritual masters of old, the need to make this distinction will become all the more evident in the face of our changed understanding of the world around us. This is because, if theology is faith seeking understanding, the language of beliefs that express that faith is largely dependent on the reigning cosmology or world-view that is prevalent at any given time. Thus, as the British theologian John A. T. Robinson's controversial 1963 book *Honest to God* put it, the three-story universe of old, with heaven above and hell below, is no longer credible, and while perhaps handy, when taken literally ends up as an obstacle to faith. But Robinson's aim of implementing the program of "demythologization" proposed by theologian Rudolph Bultmann would have a much more extensive goal than rearranging religious geography. As Robinson put, it in a newspaper interview shortly before his book's publication, "Our image of God must go." [1]

But in turn, we must ask if humans can "go" or get along without images — even an image of that mystery we have named "God"? This, I think is the crucial question raised by this book. It is also the reason for my choice of a modern rendition of Andrei Rublev's famous 15th century depiction of Christ enthroned in all his heavenly glory for the cover of this

Introduction

book — an iconic repetition of the many *Christos Pantocrator* images (Christ as ruler of the whole universe) that graced the sanctuaries of many Christian churches, especially after the Council of Nicea proclaimed Christ as "God from true God" in the year 325. Does or can such an image convey anything meaningful to humanity today?

This question is also my reason for choosing Albert Einstein, generally thought to have been the greatest scientific mind of the twentieth century, to be our protagonist in this debate. Although he was frequently asked about what he thought about God, Einstein seems to have been deliberately ambivalent about the subject. In 1928, Einstein wrote to one of his acquaintances that, contrary to what some were saying, particularly among his more outspoken religious critics, "I am not an atheist, nor do I think that one could call me a pantheist."[2] Indeed, a year before he had already described God as "a superior intelligence" or "a superior reasoning power," or even "an infinitely superior spirit that reveals itself in the little that we can comprehend in the knowable world."[3] But at the same time Einstein repeatedly said that he did not believe in what he called "a personal God"… "a God who concerns himself with the fate and doings of mankind."[4] So a major part of the problem seems to be what is meant by the word *God* to begin with. Does that word imply a person of some sort, or does it merely refer to a "first cause," a "cosmic blue-print" or some other abstraction?

In this regard Einstein might be better described as a "deist." Classical deists believed in a God who is a creator or designer of the universe, but after having done that, is a God who takes no interest in his creation. Thus the God of deism, even if in some sense a "person," does not seem to be one with whom we'd have much of a personal relationship.

Einstein and the Image of God

This ambiguity over what Einstein really meant seems to have, in turn, caused further confusion. For example, in 2013, the highly respected philosopher and legal scholar, Ronald Dworkin, on page three of his final book *Religion without God*, made the claim that "Albert Einstein said that although he was an atheist he was a deeply religious one." But Dworkin never gave a reference for this statement; apparently having confused Einstein's supposed atheism with Einstein's much later admission that when it came to the subject of God, he remained an "agnostic."[5] Yet Einstein had said as much the same when it came to understanding not only the ultimate nature of God but also of the Universe. Thus when asked about this in 1950, about five years before his death, Einstein admitted:

> We know nothing about it at all. All our knowledge is but the knowledge of school children. Possibly we shall know a little more than we do now. But the real nature of things, that we shall never know, never.[6]

This position, which may also be described as a kind of "agnosticism" (literally one of "not knowing") is a position which, as we will see in the final part of this book, was not too different than that held by some of Christianity's greatest theologians when it comes to any claims that we can know the ultimate nature of God. To be fair, however, twenty-nine pages later, Dworkin finally explained that by "God", he meant God as depicted by Michelangelo in the Sistine chapel [7] — all of which probably only confirms my friend's observation that, when it comes to someone else's idea of God, everyone is an atheist!

To understand Einstein in this whole matter, however, it is important to be reminded that Einstein as far back as 1927

Introduction

explained that he believed in "Spinoza's God" and a year later he admitted that he was fascinated by "Spinoza's pantheism."[8]

These latter statements are significant, especially in light of the well known fact that Einstein, quite early in his adult life, was very much attracted to the thought of the philosopher Spinoza. Baruch de Spinoza (1632-1677), a Jew of Portuguese descent, had been, as a young man, expelled from the synagogue in Amsterdam under the accusation that he was an atheist. At that point in his life, Spinoza moved away from Amsterdam and signaled his break with his ancestral faith by changing his Hebrew first name to its Latin equivalent, *Benedictus*. Taking up the trade of lens grinding to support himself, Spinoza devoted the rest of his short life to philosophy, particularly a philosophy that is centered on the presence of God in the world and God's part in everything that happens in it. But rather than convincing others that he was not an atheist, he only further outraged believers of all varieties by his critiques of organized religion. And after his treatise on *Ethics* was published not long after his death, his works were placed on the Index of Forbidden Books by the Catholic Church on the suspicion that he was a pantheist — which in the eyes of most believers was seen as being almost as bad as atheism.

So although he confirmed that he believed in Spinoza's God, Einstein, also a Jew, but from a non-observant family, apparently begged to differ from popular misrepresentations of Spinoza as an atheist. However, Einstein seems to have had his own peculiar set of reasons for his belief in Spinoza's God, which included his belief that Spinoza had taught that humans are completely determined by the laws of nature and thus really lack free will. In addition, even aside from that, Einstein seemed to have realized that his views about what he called his "cosmic religion" probably seemed rather beyond

Einstein and the Image of God

the comprehension of most people. Thus, as we shall see shortly in Chapter One, Einstein conceded that most people seemed to require belief in what he called "a personal God" in order to have some kind of "transcendental outlook" on life.[9]

In more than one way this string of Einstein's statements sums up the predicament addressed by this book. The fact is that, as we will see in the first chapter, this belief in a God who is disinterested, and thus not personally involved in any way with the world, was not entirely new and is shared by a large and growing segment of the American population today. In fact, in some countries, it is the prevailing view.

In some ways, this whole phenomenon might be seen as parts of the growing pains involved with the maturation of human thought. Indeed, even the so-called "New Atheism" might be seen as a kind of half-way stage or phase within the context of this whole process. If so, it is really nothing new. Those who are familiar with commentaries on, or even good footnotes to what Christians call "The Old Testament" have probably been long aware that within the seven or so centuries of their composition that there is evidence not only a of a wide range of understanding but even a growing sophistication regarding the concept of God and God's relationship to the world.

To take one obvious example, in the first several chapters of the Book of Genesis, there are not just one, but two different accounts of creation. Thus we have the oldest and more primitive account beginning in Chapter 2, contrasted to the more stately account given in the first chapter by the later authors or compilers of the various ancient stories. It was these later editors who arranged creation into seven "days", beginning with the creation of light and ending with the creation of the first humans in God's "own image and

Introduction

likeness", followed by a "day" of rest. — thus subtly suggesting that humans would be wise to do the same.

Nor did the process of refinement end there. In the centuries that followed, many of the prophets voiced strong criticism of the primitive ideas of sacrifice, as if God somehow was to be placated by the smell of burnt flesh or by the taste of fresh blood. Indeed, some would have done away with ritual sacrifice altogether: it was not Jesus who was the first to say "I want mercy, not sacrifice"[10], but the prophets Amos and Hosea even centuries before.[11]

Likewise, neither did the idea of creation through evolution begin with Darwin. Several of the pre-Socratic Greek philosophers had envisioned it, as well as Lucretius among the Romans, and St. Augustine among the early Christian theologians, who also pointed out that "the seven days of creation" were obviously a literary device and that God instead created the universe in an instant, but with the various species of life in a manner in which they would only gradually take on their present form.[12] In addition, it also was Augustine's opinion that whenever there may seem to be a conflict between the Holy Scriptures and clear and consistent rational thinking, it is a good indication that we are probably interpreting the Bible wrongly.

Centuries later, the medieval theologian, St. Bonaventure. echoed much the same when he reminded us that that there are two books of God's revelation, not just the Bible but the "Book of Nature" as well. We must, if we believe that God created the world, give equal weight to both. From this perspective, both religious fundamentalism and atheism are peas from the same pod. Indeed, as Einstein noted back in 1941 "...there are the fanatical atheists whose intolerance is the same as that of the religious fanatics, and it springs from the same source..."[13] Einstein thought that "source" was their

Einstein and the Image of God

inability "to hear the music of the spheres"[14], in other words "the Book of Nature."

However, as I hope will become clear to the reader in the second chapter of this book, the problem today lies not so much in not being able "to hear the music" or to read the Book of Nature, as being able to read between the lines of the latest edition of that book and not being able to face the music in what they are hearing. As we shall see, perhaps there was even some unwillingness on Einstein's part to admit that the universe, as we know it, will not continue to be, at least as it is now, forever. If so, Einstein was not the first. The philosopher Friedrich Nietzsche, who had announced the death of God a decade or so before Einstein discovered Spinoza's God, seemed to sense this. Otherwise, it is hard to explain Nietzsche's appeal to his theory of "eternal recurrence"[15] — his belief that after this universe is spent, another universe, in which every event, including those that have taken or will take place in the life of each and every one of us, will be repeated, and so on, over and over again, ad infinitum. Fantastic? Certainly, but is it any more so than the multiple "universes" or "multiverses" or other scenarios being cooked up by the astrophysicists and other scientists who have hitched their hopes to the "New Atheist" camp?

Nevertheless, even if we find ourselves in great sympathy with Einstein and his appeal to Spinoza's God, we still have to face the problem that Einstein recognized, that "the main source of the present day conflicts between the spheres of religion and science lies in the concept of a personal God."[16] No doubt this is true, even if we disagree in his opinion that "In their struggle for the ethical good, teachers of religion must have the stature to give up the doctrine of a personal God..."[17] How overcome this problem? That, in a nutshell, is one of the main issues faced by this book.

Introduction

The first big step into proposing a means of reconciliation between these two levels of religion — the one "personal" (in Chapter 1) and the other "cosmic" (in Chapter 2) — will be in Chapter 3, where after clearing up some misconceptions about Spinoza's ideas, I will introduce only a bit – considering the length and complexity of his major work – of the thinking of the philosopher Alfred North Whitehead. Whitehead, who was Einstein's contemporary, in many ways might be considered Spinoza's great successor, and in one major point, Spinoza's, and to some degree, also Einstein's corrector. This is because Whitehead, from the very beginning, rethought the nature of all reality, including God's role in it, in evolutionary rather than mechanistic terms. And as we will see, this makes all the difference.

One of those differences will be, in this book, the role played by Jesus, whom both Spinoza and Einstein greatly admired. In fact Einstein once admitted that he was "enthralled by the image of the Nazarene" and resisted any suggestion, still heard from some atheists today, that Jesus was a "myth."[18] Likewise, for Whitehead, who, although the son of a clergyman, never closely identified with any particular church during his adult life. In Whitehead's estimation, Jesus afforded us "the Galilean vision" of a God who cares[19], and who is even "our fellow sufferer."[20] In other words, Whitehead seems to have come close to presenting Jesus as being, for us, as described in the Epistle to the Colossians as "the image of the invisible God"[21], at least in this aspect.

Can, and if so, how does Jesus fulfill this function? And to what extent can he continue do so in view of our greatly expanded — even since the time of Einstein and Whitehead — view of the size and the fate of the universe? This is the topic of the second part of this book, which will begin in Chapter 4

Einstein and the Image of God

to assess what we actually know about the historical Jesus and compare this (in Chapter 5) to what Christian tradition and teachings have made of him in the centuries that have followed. In Chapter 6 we will take the same question one step further. Can Jesus really continue to be envisioned as the "Cosmic Christ," as he was by the Jesuit paleontologist and evolutionary thinker — and another contemporary of Einstein — Pierre Teilhard de Chardin? Can Christ really continue to serve as the focal point, or ultimate goal for the evolution of humanity, or indeed the whole universe, as Teilhard once thought?

So where does that leave us? That will be the topic of Part Three or the concluding part of this book ("Christ and the God Beyond God"). This question, in turn, leads us back to our original quandary, which even for Einstein remained unsolved, except to admit that he remained an "agnostic", both in regard to the ultimate nature of the universe as well as of God. Thus, in Chapter 7 ("Christ and the God beyond Images") where after attempting to explain my own conclusions regarding the identity of Jesus, I will turn to that more truly positive sense of that reverent agnosticism which has been the longstanding tradition of Christian theology that has been known by the tongue-twisting term *apophaticism* — literally translated, the practice of putting limits on what can be said. And if that is so, might it not also put a limit on what images, whether literary or graphic, can ever be expected to fully describe what Pope Benedict XVI called "that unknown reality that faith calls *God*."[22]

In other words, it is hoped that this concluding part will turn out to be, like all true syntheses, not just a compromise, but a conclusion that succeeds in lifting us above the current arena of scientific and religious wrangling and moving us

Introduction

more deeply into the mystery of where God and the Universe intersect.

However, it should also be added, that the opinions expressed in this book are largely my own, and that unless quoted from official documents or declarations of the Catholic Church, they represent my own conclusions or else of those of others who like me, have spent most of their life-time trying to achieve a balance between reason and faith, with a view of science that is in part inspired, rather than obstructed, by religion.

---

[1] *The Observer,* March 17, 1963.
[2] Jammer, Max. *Einstein and Religion,* 48.
[3] Calaprice, Alice. *The Ultimate Quotable Einstein,* 325.
[4] Calaprice, 324-35.
[5] Calaprice, 340.
[6] Calaprice, 344.
[7] Dworkin, Ronald. *Religion without God,* 32.
[8] Calaprice, 152.
[9] Jammer, 51.
[10] Mt 9:13; 12:7.
[11] Am 5:21; Hoes 10:11.
[12] See catholicorigins.com/st-augustine's-rationes-seminales/ (accessed 7-3-2015).
[13] Calaprice, 337.
[14] Calaprice, 337.
[15] *Thus Spake Zarathustra,* LXXIX, 9.
[16] Calaprice, 335.
[17] Calaprice, 336.
[18] Jammer, 22.

Einstein and the Image of God

[19] Whitehead, A. N., *Process and Reality*, 519.
[20] Whitehead, 532.
[21] Col 1:15.
[22] Ratzinger, Josef, *Co-workers of the Truth*, 303.

Part I
The Unknown God

The idea of idea of trying to demonstrate that this unknown exists is folly...for if God does not exist it would be of course impossible to prove it; and if he does exist it would be folly to attempt it.
(Kierkegaard)

Chapter 1
Atheism and the God of Experience

If atheism is understood as the lack of belief in God, then immediately a question comes to mind. What does one mean by the word God or gods? Maybe we think we have a clear understanding of what we are talking about, and when we look at a definition of God in Webster's we find that in monotheistic religions, God (always spelled with a capital G) is described as "... the creator and ruler of the universe, regarded as eternal, infinite, all-powerful and all-knowing; [the] Supreme Being; [the] Almighty."[1] But the range of human ideas on the subject tells another story.

For example, as far back as the 5th century BCE, the Greek philosopher Xenophanes remarked as to how he observed during his travels that each race tended to depict their God or gods with physical features resembling themselves, adding — rather cynically it seems — that "If the horses or cattle had gods, they would undoubtedly depict them as horses or cattle." St. Clement of Alexandria, a 3rd century Christian theologian, claimed that Xenophanes also taught that the only true God would have no physical shape whatsoever. However, if Xenophanes did, apparently that fragment of his writing is now missing.

Much later, in the 13th century of our own era, the theologian St. Thomas Aquinas noted, in much more ponderous tones, "Whatever is received is received according to the mode of the recipient."[2] In other words, we tend to form our ideas, or really, our images — since these tend to come first — from our own personal experience of things.

This is true even when we learn of things second-hand, that is, when someone else tells us about something that has

Einstein and the Image of God

happened or about an idea that they might have. And, if from their words or descriptions we still are unable to imagine or picture what they are saying, we are apt to say that we just "don't get it" or some other expression of our incomprehension.

Furthermore, and it is very important that we always remember this — especially when it comes to certain subjects, like God — that almost inevitably experience, whether first-hand or second-hand, generally trumps thinking. Or to put it another way, unless we take extra measures to prevent it, our "heart" or emotion tends overwhelm our brain. And if this is true about the subject of God in general, it is even all the more true when one is discussing whether or not God is in some way a "person".

To better understand this we are going to be looking at several studies on the subject, one of them based on psychological theory, another based on a sociological survey and still another, a land-mark text on the subject of religious experience. All these tend to confirm that, when it comes to the subject of God, our first–hand impressions or even later religious experiences tend to outweigh or override any philosophical reasoning or theological pondering on the subject.

A. Freud and the "Father-Figure" as God

In his 1927 book on religion, titled *The Future of an Illusion*, Sigmund Freud, the father of modern psychoanalysis, mentioned at least a half a dozen times that people's notion of God, or even the origin of religion itself, is connected to what he called "the father-figure". The book was apparently widely read, and even Einstein commented upon it, expressing his doubt that Freud's belief that mankind should get rid of this fixation or illusion would be a good idea. As he wrote in a

Atheism and the God of Experience

letter in 1928 to someone who was asking Einstein about his own beliefs:

> It is a different question whether belief in a personal God should be contested. Freud in his most recent book endorsed this view... I myself would never engage in such a task. For such a belief seems to me preferable to any lack of any transcendental outlook of life, and I wonder whether one can ever successfully render to the majority of mankind a more sublime means in order to satisfy its metaphysical needs.[3]

While Freud seems to have never actually followed up his "father-figure" theory with any hard statistical data or even case studies from his own practice, the American psychologist Paul Vitz decided to try to do so, starting with some testing and sampling he began doing while still a undergraduate student at the University of Michigan back in the 1950s. After graduating from Stanford with a Ph.D., Vitz went on to become a notable critic of modern culture, not even sparing his own academic field with a book titled *Psychology as Religion: The Cult of Self Worship*, first published in 1977.

In a book he titled *Faith of the Fatherless: The Psychology of Atheism* that was published in 1999, Vitz followed up on Freud's theory, comparing about a dozen or so famous figures, some atheists and others believers, concluding that that it does seem that either tyrannical or else weak, or even totally absent fathers appear to correlate with the occurrence of atheism in their children, while having had a strong and loving father seems to favor continued faith in God. Vitz then went on to describe how having had a strong and loving father, he eventually drew him back from his own late adolescent atheism and brought him to embrace the Catholic faith.

Einstein and the Image of God

However, one wonders if, without much more extensive research on the subject, Vitz's conclusions, if drawn mainly from the lives of about a dozen notable or famous persons including Nietzsche (dead father) and Freud (weak father), necessarily hold true as a general rule. But if one considers how frightening people find many of the depictions of God to have been, particularly some of those found in what Christians call "the Old Testament", this would certainly seem to explain Einstein's rejection, not of his Jewish identity, or even of God as such, but of the image of God as a "person" who judges or answers prayers. Yet his admiration for the figure of Jesus — a pattern that we will also see in the thought of philosopher Benedict Spinoza, Einstein's intellectual hero — seems to overlook the fact that Jesus, for all his depictions of God as his "Father" and his teaching his followers to address God as "Our Father", could also sometimes warn us that this same "Father" might at times exercise what we have more recently come to call "tough love".

In the sixth chapter of the newer edition of his book, Vitz also adds some more recent research, mostly by a Dr. Baron-Cohen in Great Britain, which seems to indicate a certain correlation between atheism, agnosticism, and autism, associated with "a particularly intense drive to systematize and an unusually low drive to empathize". Walter Issacson also notes the same findings in his recent biography of Einstein and goes on in a long endnote to comment how this finding has been seized upon as an encouraging sign for parents of small boys diagnosed with Asperger's Syndrome.[4] Issacson, however, disagrees with Baron-Cohen, pointing out that even as a boy, Einstein easily made friends. Nevertheless, Vitz does go on to point out other studies that also tend to correlate male thinking patterns not so much with atheism,

Atheism and the God of Experience

but with abstract or impersonal concepts of God – something that certainly describes Einstein's thinking.

In any case, with all this Freudian emphasis on God primarily as "Our Father", we can't help but wonder if that explains, at least in part, the growing popularity of feminist theology in some Christian churches, or the even the long-standing popularity of devotion to the Blessed Virgin Mary or "the Mother of God" among so many more-traditional Christians, especially among the Roman Catholic and Eastern Orthodox churches. But this diversity among views of God as "Father" leads us next to a sociological study that seems to be based less on psychological theory and more on statistical facts.

B: America's Four Gods

It turns out that even your average believer in God is not all that likely to have the identical idea of God as other "average believers". In fact, in a 2008 Gallup Poll commissioned by Baylor University's Institute for Studies in Religion, it turned out that, despite all the publicity surrounding atheism and "the New Atheists", only 5% of a wide sample of Americans taken from many different regions of the United States classified themselves as atheists. But even about half of these were not even certain about that, being merely doubters or agnostics regarding whether there really is a God.

Furthermore, it seems that when the 95% who classified themselves as being believers (which includes those who prefer to describe themselves as "spiritual" rather than "religious") were asked questions about how or what they thought about God, it became evident their concepts of God varied widely — especially when questioned about two crucial issues. The first issue was concerning whether or not they saw God as being *engaged* or caring about the world or

Einstein and the Image of God

what happens in it. The second issue was whether or not God is *judgmental* — that is, whether they thought God would hold them or others responsible for their conduct and will reward or punish them accordingly.

Depending on the answers to these two main questions, four possible combinations resulted, each so distinct that the authors named their study *America's Four Gods*, adding, as a subtitle, *What We Say About God and What That Says About Us*. Accordingly, we will be following their analysis, both in terms of the various ideas people have about God, particularly when regarded as something like a "person", and what motivations or influences may have shaped these particular ideas or images.

1: The "Authoritative God"

Thirty-one percent said they believed in what the authors call an "Authoritative God", a God who is both *engaged* in the world and who is *judgmental* — in other words, a God who will hold us to account as to how we have lived our lives. In America, where, according to a 2012 Gallup Poll, 77% of the population still considers itself to be Christian, this also includes belief in the Hebrew Scriptures — in Christian terms, the "Old Testament" — on which great emphasis is placed, especially in America's Bible Belt, where fundamentalist religious views still remain strong. Given these statistics, it is also not too remarkable that such a view tends to predominate, according to the Baylor study, among white American males, among whom the "law and order" political mentality also holds sway. It also seems to fit the Freudian thesis, where we would expect male offspring to model themselves after their *fathers*, who in conservative societies, are expected to be the disciplinarians, laying down the law and enforcing it.

Atheism and the God of Experience

2: The "Benevolent God"
If the above is true, then it is hardly surprising that women tend to predominate among the 24% who see God as being "benevolent" — a description combining the traits of being engaged but also forgiving or non-judgmental. This would be because, in Freudian terms, it might seem logical to suppose that women perhaps take their image of God more from their mother than their father, providing that their mother was the more loving and understanding parent. Such a situation might also be seen as a possible explanation, at least in part, for the insistence, by feminist theologians, that we rethink our habit of referring to God as a "He" and give the designation "She" equal time to the divinity — even though it may raise the specter of long-forgotten goddesses or even a revival of the Wiccan worship of *Gaia* as Mother Earth. If not anything else, however, this longing for a more feminine image of God probably explains a penchant for a substitute "Sweet Jesus" brand of piety in contrast to an overly-demanding and strict Father-God.

3: The "Critical God"
According to the Baylor study, 16% of the population sees God as being "Critical", that is to say, a God who is judgmental, yet not all that much engaged. This view is most often found among minorities, especially Blacks and Hispanics, who together make up a very large and vocal portion of America's poor underclass. If so, then should we be surprised that they have strong ideas of what a just society should look like but are sorely disappointed when they find their hopes and prayers, as well as their demands for a more just and egalitarian society, unanswered?

Einstein and the Image of God

While this segment of American society may still be statistically a minority, their situation and the attitude it fosters also raises a major question that has proved a stumbling block, not only for those in the next group to be considered, but as we will see in the next chapter, has, for many others, raised a complete barrier to belief in any kind of God. For if someone thinks of God as judgmental, but not engaged, it is easy to see why they also might end up angry or mad at God for not intervening to bring about justice. But for someone who falls into the next category, it is not a huge step to wonder if there is a God to begin with.

4: The "Distant God"

Finally, and seen as perhaps most significant by the analysts, another 24% said that for them God is "Distant", a God who is both non-judgmental and disengaged. In addition, they found that for many of those among that portion of the 5% who had already classified themselves as agnostics, but not necessarily as convinced atheists, this description fits their idea of a God — if there is one — particularly the part about being "disengaged". In other words, if the Gallup organization's statistics can be trusted, it seems that nearly a quarter of the population of the United States holds a view of God, which although perhaps not as exalted or expressive, is not all that much different from that held by some of America's founding fathers, who despite their nominal Christianity, held the more philosophical view of God that became known as "Deism". It tends to view God as the "Grand Architect" of a clock-work like universe, who had designed it and built it, but then had, for all practical purposes, turned his back on it and walked away, leaving it to fend on its own.

Since this book has been written especially with such a view of a "distant" God in mind, we will, of course, be taking

Atheism and the God of Experience

a closer look at this outlook in the next chapter, as well as the reasoning behind it, and the effect it has on our lives. But for now, since our focus has been on our perceptions or impressions of God, rather than on abstract thinking or reasoning, it probably suffices to point out that such a "Distant God" is one that tends to relieve us entirely from having to deal with God as a "person" or what Einstein called a "personal God". Yet at the same time, this ambiguity in Einstein's own choice of terms —he confessed that he was never comfortable with his limited command of the English language — it raises a further question. Is it possible to have any concept of God as a "person" without in some way having had a personal religious experience of some sort?

Frankly, it doesn't seem so. But this does not mean that personal religious experience will necessarily result in a sense of God as a person. Instead, God may be experienced simply as a power, a presence, a feeling of awe, such as Einstein himself expressed when in a letter he wrote back in 1927, he explained:

> I cannot conceive of a personal God who would directly influence the actions of individuals....My religiosity consists of a humble admiration of the infinitely superior spirit that reveals itself in the little that we can comprehend of the knowable world. That deeply emotional conviction of the presence of a superior reasoning power, which is revealed in the incomprehensible universe, forms my idea of God.[5]

And again, two years later, in a letter to a rabbi that was published in the *New York Times*, Einstein replied:

> I believe in Spinoza's God, Who reveals Himself in the lawful harmony of the world, not in a God who concerns himself with the fate and doings of mankind.[6]

Einstein and the Image of God

However, as has been pointed out more than once, because Einstein did not believe that God concerns himself with human affairs, neither answering prayers, nor punishing them for their misbehavior, people have accused Einstein, as they once did Spinoza, of being an atheist, even though both of them denied it. The same goes for the charge of *pantheism*, a view which Spinoza denied, but which Einstein admitted in 1923 that "in common terms, one can describe it as 'pantheistic'"[7], only to question a few years later "if I can define myself as a pantheist."[8] We will be seeing more exactly how Spinoza understood God in Chapter 3, and whether or not Einstein correctly understood Spinoza. But for now we'll have to pass on to a much broader spectrum of religious experience and it implications.

C: Varieties of Religious Experience

Back in 1902, the American psychologist and philosopher, William James, published a series of lectures that he had been invited to give at the University of Edinburgh, under the title *The Varieties of Religious Experience*. This book, with its pragmatic approach, has probably influenced more thought on the phenomenon of religion, not as a history of institutions, but as a mode of knowledge or relating to the world than anything that has ever been published since.

The most famous, or well-known phenomenon discussed in James' study is the distinction between what he called the "once-born" believer and the "twice-born". The first category refers to persons who have grown up, usually from early childhood, in a religious faith in which they have gradually matured and generally remained content in the tradition first imparted to them. The second category, the "twice-born" refers to those who may have been, as was usual back in

Atheism and the God of Experience

James' life-time, reared in an inherited religious tradition, but who, sometime later in life, have undergone a conversion experience of some sort — hence the expression "born-again Christian" that we've heard about so much in recent times. For some, this experience meant a switch in religious denomination, often from a more traditional established or main-line "Church" to a more charismatic, free-style congregation.

For others, this "conversion" simply means that they have finally reached a stage in life where they have come to realize that they must begin to take their inherited faith more seriously and do so in a way that affects their daily life. In more recent times, extensive studies have been made in this area of religious psychology, particularly by theologian James W. Fowler, who has built on the early work of developmental psychologist Erik Erikson, educational psychologist Jean Piaget, and the stages of moral development as described by Lawrence Kohlberg. Fowler mapped out six distinct "Stages of Faith" in his 1981 book by that title. But, after he realized the importance of basic trust during infancy, Fowler added a new beginning stage to result in a total of seven stages in his 1984 sequel which was pointedly titled *Becoming Adult, Becoming Christian: Adult Development and Christian Life* — which would certainly seem to imply that one cannot really be the latter until one has reached a certain level of maturity. Likewise even Einstein had his own belief that religion passed through at least three stages, beginning with a religion based on a primitive fear of nature, gradually supplanted by a more social stage focused on interpersonal ethics, and this, in turn, to be finally supplanted by his own brand of "cosmic religion."[9]

In another book on the same subject, I have suggested, on the basis of Viktor Frankl's analysis of psychodynamics, that such growth into an adult stage, rather than remaining tied to childish stages of faith, is not possible unless one can overcome one's own security needs.[10]

Such a discussion of faith stages and becoming "born again" of course raises the question of whether a loss of faith or renouncement of religious beliefs might not sometimes itself be seen as a necessary step to achieve full adulthood. Freud, whose ideas we have already seen, seems to have thought so. But surprisingly, at least some authorities on the spiritual life also seem to think so, but for quite the opposite reasons being touted by the "New Atheists". Some of these, much like those atheists Einstein had already noted years ago, seem to display the same sort of mentality as found in the worst religious fanatics.[11]

In terms of the faith stages mapped out by James Fowler, this sort of aggressive atheism often shows all the same signs that tend to characterize the kind of adolescent rebellion that is characteristic of a movement from a purely conventional stage of faith dominated by ones own family, class values, and authority figures, to a more personal stage of self-determination. However, one of the dangers of this transition, due to the threatening feelings of insecurity, is the temptation to revert to an even earlier stage of thinking, one dominated by a kind of religious fundamentalism or, its modern counterpart, the kind of scientific reductionism once called "positivism" but now described more as "scientism". When this happens, it becomes almost impossible for a person to ever progress to what might be called a "conjunctive" state of faith, one that, in Fowler's words:

> ...emerges with mid-life or beyond [and] involves the integration of elements in ourselves, in society, and our experience of ultimate reality that have the character of

Atheism and the God of Experience

apparent contradictions, polarities, or at least paradoxical elements.[12]

It seems that when that conjunctive stage, or what Fowler described as a "paradoxical-consolidative faith", has not been reached, any further progress in spiritual growth to a final "universalizing" or "Unitative Faith" is blocked, unless a rather drastic psycho-spiritual upheaval takes place. Thus the Czech priest-psychologist Tomáš Halik, who grew up as an atheist in Europe's most atheistic country, has pointed out that the 16th century Spanish theologian and mystic, St. John of the Cross, spoke of a "Dark Night of the Soul" as being a necessary stage before a person can achieve full union with God.[13] Even before that, the unknown author of the 14th century English book, *The Cloud of Unknowing,* based on ideas from an even older Eastern Christian tradition, taught that all our ideas or beliefs about God have to be negated or purified before faith can reach its final and most mature stage.

D: Personhood Reexamined: Can It Apply to God?

Much like the definition of God that we took from Webster's Dictionary, Christian ideas of God, to begin with, never explicitly spoke of God as a "person" or discussed what is meant or even implied by the term "personhood". In fact, the first recorded Christian use of the term *persona* as applied to God was not by a theologian, but by the North African lawyer Tertullian (160-225), who devoted much time to making his case for Christianity. Tertullian was the first to speak about God being manifested, as it were, not simply as one but as in the form of three *personae* or "persons".

But we tend to forget that in Tertullian's time the Latin word *persona* still literally meant an actor's mask — something through (*per*) sound (*sona*) passed, thus having much the same

Einstein and the Image of God

connotation as the Greek *prosōpon*, which meant a "countenance" or "face". It was only later on, during the 6th century, that the Christian philosopher, Boethius (480-524), attempted to define "person" in anything like exact terms. But, this having been fifteen centuries ago, his definition may sound rather strange to modern ears. As Boethius put it: "A person is an individual substance of a rational nature."[14]

We will see this word "substance" used in a similar way later when we look at Spinoza's definition of God, as well as Einstein's understanding or possible misunderstanding of the same. But for the time being, let us note that, unlike our present understanding of that word, which we tend to equate with physical matter or any material stuff, "substance" literally means whatever it is that "stands" (Latin verb *sto, stare*) "beneath" or "below" (Latin *sub*) whatever is at the surface. In other words, what Boethius was talking about is a deeper or more basic reality than what meets our eyes. Thus, the present dictionary definition of a person as "an individual human being" refers to something much more basic than mere "personality" or outward appearance or characteristics. It has to do with the fundamental nature of that being and its intrinsic value or worth.

So, once we understand the word "person" in this more philosophical sense, can we, or should we apply it to God? In Chapter 4 of Book VII in his treatise on the Trinity, St Augustine discusses the analogical use of language, including the use of the word "person" when used regarding God, a question which was taken up again centuries later by Thomas Aquinas. According to Aquinas, since the word "Person" signifies "what is most perfect in all nature" it is "fittingly applied to God" as "His essence contains every perfection." However, it is not to be applied to God "as it is applied to creatures, but in a more excellent way..."[15]

Atheism and the God of Experience

On the other hand, Karl Rahner, generally thought to have been the greatest Catholic theologian of the 20th century, believed that the common understanding of God as a trinity of three *persons* is deeply misleading, and that there should be a moratorium on that use of the word "person". As Rahner put it, Christians must be clearly seen, to the rest of the world, as monotheists or believers in one God in line with the whole biblical tradition and not, as Rahner pointed out, is too often unfortunately the case, as "tritheists".[16] Likewise, as a result of the same problem, some contemporary Christian authors have come out with books with titles like *The Three Faces of God*[17] or *Jesus, the Human Face of God.*[18]

Likewise, Max Jammer also points out that while the Protestant theologian Paul Tillich, while arguing that the idea of God as a person is a necessary "symbol" for our understanding of God and is altogether "indispensable for a living religion"— that it is *only* a representation" which like the word "God" itself "transcend[s] its own conceptual content."[19] Similarly, in discussing Einstein's views, the Catholic theologian Hans Küng also pointed out that "God is not a person as man is a person…The term 'person' also is merely a cipher for God."[20]

Tillich's and Küng's opinions would also appear to support, in turn, some remarks about God as a trinity that the retired American Episcopal Bishop John Shelby Spong made on his website a few years ago.[21] As Spong put it, when we experience God "as the source of life beyond limit that the human imagination can impose on anything" we tend to call him "Father". And when we experience God "as the ultimate depth of life, deeper than our own breath…we call that dimension of life 'Spirit'." And when we experience God "coming to us through the lives of others, and especially for those of us who are Christians, coming to us uniquely through

Einstein and the Image of God

the life of one called Jesus of Nazareth... we name him 'Son', offspring of 'the Father'." Spong concluded that while he really doesn't know whether or not God is a trinity, he nevertheless believes that whenever humans try to think about God, they tend to end up thinking in a kind of Trinitarian pattern.

What Spong has observed on the phenomenological level has been more amply confirmed, on the metaphysical level, by the more traditional orthodox thinker, philosopher David Bentley Hart in his book *The Experience of God*[22], and by the ecumenical theologian, Raimon Panikkar, who in his 1989 Gifford lectures, published as *The Rhythm of Being: The Unbroken Trinity*, focused even more on insights from the East.[23]

Conclusion

All that we have considered so far would seem to boil down to four main observations or findings. The first observation is that most likely Freud was guessing correctly when he theorized that our personal ideas or images of God have very deep roots, so deep that they probably reach back to our unconscious level that controls our imagination and emotions.

The second finding, based on the Baylor University study of religious beliefs in the United States, would seem to confirm Freud's guess, and that in general terms, reveals a variety of images of God that fall into more or less four different patterns, the last of which ("The Distant God") appears to represent a considerable portion of the population. It also seems to border on a small, but yet growing segment of society that considers itself to be, if not convinced atheists, somewhat agnostic on the question.

As a third factor, the classic study of the process of religious conversion described by psychologist and philosopher William James, has led us further into the

Atheism and the God of Experience

recognition of how much the patterns of general human psychological development affect religious faith, particularly in terms of adherence to certain beliefs.

Finally, taking all these findings into consideration, it is probably safe to say, as was said in the beginning, that how we perceive or experience God or our idea of God overrides any efforts at abstract thinking on the subject. For those who are fearful or anxious, God will be seen as an exacting or demanding God, while for those who are angry, God will be seen as a wrathful God. And for those who acquire a loving heart, well, for them, at least most of the time, "God is love."[24] This, in turn, means that for most persons who believe in a God, God is personal, and thus is thought of as a "person" or is experienced by them in terms somewhat analogous to personhood. Not that this is universal, but as we have already seen in our prime example of this difficulty, the case of Albert Einstein, that even he could not seem to avoid speaking of God as if God is a person, even while he repeatedly denied that he believed that God actually is one. Nor can we it seems, given the constraints of human language, like Einstein, avoid speaking as if God is a person, particularly if we have had any personal experience of the Transcendent.

---

[1] *Webster's New Universal Unabridged Dictionary*, New York, Simon & Schuster, 1979.
[2] *Summa Theologica*, Part I, Q.75, A.5; Q.76, A.2; Q.89, A.5; Part III, Q.54, A.2.
[3] Jammer, Max, *Einstein and Religion*, 23.
[4] Isaacson, *Einstein: His Life and Universe*, 15, 566 n15.
[5] Calaprice, Alice. *The Ultimate Quotable Einstein*, 325.
[6] Calaprice, 325.
[7] Calaprice, 324.

[8] Calaprice, 326.
[9] Einstein, Albert, *The World as I See It*, 23-28.
[10] Kropf, Richard W. *Faith, Security, and Risk*, 1990.
[11] Calaprice, 337.
[12] Fowler, James, W. *The Stages of Faith*, 1984, 64.
[13] Halik, Tomáš *The Night of the Confessor*, 2012, 19.
[14] *"Persona est rationalis naturae individualis substantia"* (*De duabis naturis*, 1).
[15] *Summa Theologica,* Part I, Q. 29, A.3.
[16] Rahner, Karl. *The Trinity*, 42-43; *Encyclopedia of Theology*, 1755-64.
[17] Miller, David L. *The Three Faces of God*, 2005.
[18] Parini, Jay. *Jesus, the Human Face of God*, 2013.
[19] Jammer, 112-13.
[20] Jammer, 113.
[21] https://johnshelbyspong.com/2011/08/18/lecturing-in-the-church-of-scotland/#comments (accessed 5/15/2014).
[22] Hart, David Bentley, *The Experience of God*, 2013.
[23] Panikkar, Raimon, *The Rhythm of Being*, 2010.
[24] 1 John 4:16.

Chapter 2
Science and the God of Reason

If we are to take seriously what we saw about religious experience, then we must also take seriously the warning of psychologist and philosopher William James that religious experiences are usually only convincing to those who have actually had them. And it is for this reason that, as he explained (in Chapter 18, titled "Philosophy") of his landmark book on the *Varieties of Religious Experience*, that there are basically two approaches to a philosophical study of religion. One is to attempt to construct a rational foundation for belief, or (as Webster's describes it in its definition of "Theology") "the study of God and the relationship between God and the universe; the study of religious doctrines and matters of divinity." The other is to study the phenomenon of religion, looking at the commonalities that make all religions similar, despite difference in beliefs — something that James called "a Science of Religion." What this chapter is about is the first approach, the purpose of which James described in the following words:

> To find an escape from obscure and wayward personal persuasion to truth objectively valid for all thinking men has ever been the intellect's most cherished ideal. To redeem religion from unwholesome privacy, and to give public status and right of way to its deliverances, has been reason's task.[1]

And as James went on to say, this task has been unending. But as he observed some pages later, the results have been inconclusive. As James saw it:

Einstein and the Image of God

The arguments for God's existence have stood for hundreds of years with the waves of unbelieving criticism breaking against them, never totally discrediting them in the ears of the faithful, but on the whole slowly and surely washing out the mortar from between their joints. If you already have a God whom you believe in, these arguments confirm you. If you are atheistic, they fail to set you right. The proofs are various. The "cosmological" one so-called, reasons from the contingence of the world to a First Cause which must contain whatever perfections the world itself contains. The "argument from design" reasons, from the fact that Nature's laws are mathematical, and her parts benevolently adapted to each other, that this cause is both intellectual and benevolent. The "moral argument" is that the moral law presupposes a lawgiver. The "argument ex consensus gentium" is that belief in God is so widespread as to be grounded in the rational nature of man, and should therefore carry authority with it.[2]

In the pages following that summary of arguments, James (who has been claimed by atheists to be one of their own, but who never openly admitted it) went on to criticize most of these arguments, not so much in detail but nevertheless quite effectively, especially concluding that the arguments from the physical structure of the universe are "easily susceptible of interpretation as arbitrary human products" and "will be convincing only to those who on other grounds believe in him already."[3]

All that being said, it might be a surprise to know that a century later, no less than a pope had also concluded that there is no absolute "proof" either in favor of there being a God or, on the other hand, that one can prove there is not one. Instead, it is a matter of whether or not one chooses what seems to be the more reasonable explanation for the way

Science and the God of Reason

things are. Thus, according to Josef Ratzinger (a.k.a. Pope Benedict XVI):

> The more we can delve into the world with our intelligence, the more clearly the plan of creation appears. In the end to reach the definitive question I would say: God exists or he does not exist. There are only two options. Either one recognizes the priority of reason, of creative Reason that is at the beginning of all things and is the principle of all things — the priority of reason is also the priority of freedom — or one holds the priority of the irrational, inasmuch as everything that functions on our earth and in our lives would only be accidental, marginal, an irrational result — reason would be a product of irrationality. One cannot ultimately "prove" either project, but the great option of Christianity is the option for rationality and for the priority of reason. This seems to be an excellent option, which shows us that behind everything is a great Intelligence to which we can trust ourselves...[4]

The thing that is so striking about this more or less informal statement by the pope, who, before he was elected pope, was the church's chief doctrinal overseer and enforcer, is that he presents belief in God as an option, or as a choice. He admitted that there is no hard and fast "proof" that can compel one to choose belief in God, or on the other hand, to choose its opposite, atheism. Instead he only appealed to what seems to us, in terms of our own powers of rationality, to choose what seems most reasonable. It is, in essence, the same line of approach that was used by Einstein in defense of what he called his "cosmic religion." But it is also, one might note, an argument that has to come to grips with some scientific facts that were unknown back in James' day and

Einstein and the Image of God

which became evident only in the last few decades of Einstein's own lifetime.

A. Being and Existence

The first of these facts is that, as far as science can tell us, the universe had a beginning. The evidence of this event was the result of observations made back in the 1920s by astronomer Edmund Hubble. Up until Hubble's time most everyone, including scientists like Einstein, believed that the universe, even though it may undergo change, had nevertheless always existed. Not only scientists, as well as philosophers like Plato and Aristotle, took this for granted, but even the Bible, starting with the second verse of the first chapter of the book of Genesis, which seems to have assumed that God created the world out of some kind of preexisting matter.[5] Likewise, the Book of Wisdom or "Wisdom of Solomon" speaks of the world being shaped from "formless matter" — words very reminiscent of those found in Plato's *Timaeus*.[6]

As to the contrary, only a passage in the Second Book of Maccabees says that "God did not make them [i.e., everything] out of things that existed."[7] So while Genesis seems to suggest some kind of pre-existing matter, Second Maccabees seems to have been the earliest place in scripture where we can find an explicit concept of *creation*, not just as shaping or designing things from something else, but literally making something from absolutely *nothing*. And it probably has been this combination of reasoning, intuition, and plain common sense, which has led to the philosophical adage, first expressed by the philosopher Parmenides around the end of the sixth century BCE that "Nothing can come from nothing." So where did all this, the universe and all that it contains, come from?

Science and the God of Reason

Today, as a result of Hubble's discoveries and further refinements in observational techniques, it is almost universally accepted that our universe began about 13.8 billion years ago. It began with a tremendous burst of energy nicknamed "the Big Bang" by the Cambridge astronomer, Fred Hoyle. Hoyle spent most of the latter part of his life trying to disprove the theory, only to grudgingly admit he was wrong, especially after the cosmic background radiation was mapped by orbiting satellite detection in 1995.[8] Even Einstein, who at times could be quite stubborn, took about four years to admit that he had been wrong in assuming the universe always existed, even after Hubble's discoveries seemed to indicate that this was not so, and thus confirmed Lemaître's theory of the universe developing from the explosion of a "primal atom," which Lemaître first proposed back in 1924. And as for the idea of a cyclical or recycling universe or one of repeated big bangs — something else that Hoyle and his colleagues toyed with — that idea also has been largely cast aside. According to cosmologist Laurence Krauss, as he repeats several times in his popular book, *A Universe from Nothing*, the universe, in terms of its expansion rate, is virtually "flat," which means that as far as anyone can tell, the universe will continue to expand as long as time lasts.[9] But with this continuing expansion, comes, according to the principle of *entropy* (Second Law of Thermodynamics) the gradual disappearance of any additional "free energy" to support life. Thus, the grim title of Krauss' Chapter 7: "Our Miserable Future." If so, then, although it may have had a long history in many ancient cultures, this mounting evidence would seem to be the death-knell for Nietzsche's dream of "eternal recurrence."

Einstein and the Image of God

All this only brings us back to the question of what caused the Big Bang. Believers in God, of course, are apt to say that God caused it. Non-believers, on the other hand, seem to have come up with two other options. Either other universes (sometimes called a "multiverse") which we can't see or detect, at least for now, or else some kind of "quantum vacuum" which, as vacuums being what they are, apparently we can't ever expect to detect, no matter how hard we look for it.

However, more recently with the realization that about 68% of the energy in the universe is the so-called "dark energy" ("dark" because its nature and origin is unknown), more and more cosmologists have turned their attention to the possibility that Einstein's 1916 speculations about the existence of gravitational waves might shed new light on the structure and dynamics of the universe. For example, Paul Steinhardt of Princeton has been trying to revive the idea of a "cyclic universe" with the help of string theory in which case the universe (in the singular) would be seen as recycling itself over periods of trillions, rather than billions, of years.[10] According to Steinhardt, the crucial evidence would be found in whether or not the "gravity waves" predicted by Einstein would ever be discovered. If they were, as was claimed back in March 2014 by an American team working at the South Pole, this would be taken as a sign of other universes. If not, as was concluded by a European team studying data from the Planck Orbiting Observatory some months later, then, according to Steinhardt, the theory of a cyclical universe would remain viable. But, early in February 2016, it was announced that the LIGO (Laser Interferometer Gravitational-wave Observatory) experiment, operating from two widely spaced locations in the USA (Louisiana and Washington state)

Science and the God of Reason

had simultaneously detected gravity waves that appear to have been generated by the merger of two black holes located about 1.3 billion light years away – well within our own universe. What this means for either Steinhardt's theory or its competitors still remains to be seen.[11]

Meanwhile, either way, apparently we have to take it on faith: either the universe has been caused by a God whom we can't ever expect to see, at least in this life, or by something else that we can't see either — although this apparently doesn't dim hopes that some day science will somehow reveal it. In either case, despite books claiming otherwise, you have a belief that something (the world or the whole universe), despite the title of Krauss' book, didn't come from nothing.

This is important, because the theological concept of God is not simply that of a "First Cause" or a "Prime Mover" (as Aristotle, since he believed the universe, in some form or another had always existed). More importantly and more fundamentally God is (as St. Augustine described it) "Being" as such or "Being in itself." This point is so important that (as some insist), it is not accurate to say that "God exists." This is because, taken literally, the word "exist"[12], implies a dependence on or relationship to, or apartness from something or someone else. Thus God simply "is", and everything else that is, is only because it "exists" – which is to say that it depends on something else, in this case God, for its existence. This fine chopping of language may seem excessive, but otherwise, the pundits say that without it we will miss what is meant by the word "God" in the first place or even end up in thinking like a small child asking "But Daddy, who made God?" In other words, without this concept of God as absolute *Being* in or of itself, we end up only caught in an infinite regression.[13]

Einstein and the Image of God

Thus this idea of God's *being* the source of all other beings is absolutely fundamental. Without it we end up answering nothing. The fact that we can't explain the basic concept of God in any other way, should not surprise us. As the British philosopher, and lifelong atheist, Anthony Flew, asserted against the evangelical theologian William Craig in 1999:

> We have to accept the Big Bang itself as the fundamental brute fact. For it is a necessary truth that all systems of scientific explanation have to end in something which explains but which itself is not explained.[14]

But within a few years, Flew realized that the same statement also could apply to God, and in 2004 admitted that he had become a "deist," and in 2007 authorized a book to be published, the title of which announced that *There is a God*, along with the rather sensational subtitle, *How the World's Most Notorious Atheist Changed His Mind*.

B: Design Revisited

Whether Flew actually really was the world's most notorious atheist — it seems that the highly publicized "New Atheists" are strongly contending among themselves for that title — Flew's "conversion" and his final book caused no little consternation. Angry reviews appeared in various publications, some suggesting that he was in severe mental decline (he died at age 87 in 2010) and that his collaborator in producing that final book, Roy A. Varghese, had taken advantage of this to promote his own ideas, a charge that Flew denied.

However, there seems that Flew's explanation as to why his view had changed caused some confusion, especially

Science and the God of Reason

when he seemed to focus on the question of the origin of life. According to Flew, who quoted various scientific authorities on the subject, not just the sheer complexity of the DNA structure (about 3 billion "bits" of information found in each and every living cell) and their duplication in transmission, but, even more, the translation of this code into RNA, constitutes an insurmountable challenge to all the proposed theories of *abiogenesis* or how life might emerge from non-life. This is because, according to Flew's sources, none of the existing theories could be fitted into a 13-14 billion year time-span that cosmologists allow for the development of the universe to its present state.[15]

To many of his critics, Flew's reasoning on this particular point seemed to be repeating the arguments of those who advocate "Intelligent Design," which they see as being nothing more than the latest disguise of creationist views held by religious fundamentalists. But after over a half a century of being one of Great Britain's best known philosophers and outspoken atheists, it is impossible to imagine how Flew's conversion to what he called "Aristotle's God" — he made it clear that he was not becoming a Christian — could have been based on creationist biblical fundamentalism.

Aside from the issue of whether Flew's reasoning on this particular issue was correct or not, the real problem, in all the debate about "Intelligent Design," is specifying exactly how the implied "Designer" (God) actually operates. If one means by this that God, at specific times, had to specially intervene to create the first forms of life or perhaps again, the first human life, a convinced evolutionist, even a religiously believing one, might rightly question if the Designer really is as intelligent as one might like to think. If, on the other hand, the whole plan according to which evolution occurred already

Einstein and the Image of God

had built into it the mechanism in which life and intelligence would eventually appear, this is quite another matter — one to which only a die-hard atheist could object. Unfortunately, Flew's final book appears to give the impression of that interventionist point of view rather than the more fully integral evolutionary one.

This is doubly unfortunate considering all the appeals and references Flew's book made to Einstein's thought. In fact, Einstein's name appears about sixty times in the book, almost all of them in respect to Einstein's emphasis on the superior intelligence or mind that is so evident in the structure and workings of the universe at large. And in turn, Einstein's views would seem to have favored a much broader view of the design argument which is mentioned, but only rather briefly, in Chapter Six of Flew's book. This is the debate over the so-called "Anthropic Principle," which is the idea that the universe was in some way designed for us, that is, the human species, to eventually appear.

The "anthropic" argument was presented, in its most complete form, by the British theoretical physicist John Barrow and the American mathematical physicist Frank Tipler, in their monumental book *The Anthropic Cosmological Principle*, which was published in 1988. The term "cosmological" in the title is crucial to their argument. This argument, after much discussion and a considerable amount of mathematical calculations regarding the various properties of the universe, comes down to basically one fact. It is that any significant variation in the basic laws of physics and the way the universe has developed, for example, the "cosmological constant" or expansion rate of the universe from the Big Bang onward, would have resulted in a universe that would have either expanded so rapidly that it would

Science and the God of Reason

have exhausted all its energy before life could have occurred, or, on the other hand, expanded so slowly that it would have collapsed upon itself. Either way, the universe would have ended with much the same result, that is, that no life, at least life as complex as ours, could have developed.

This crucial realization, perhaps, it should be pointed out again, was unknown back in 1903, when William James delivered his masterful summary and critique of the arguments quoted earlier in this chapter. Nor was it available to Einstein until Edmund Hubble's research and Lemaître's reasoning finally convinced him that his belief that the universe had always existed and would remain essentially the same had been mistaken. As a result of this new information, according to physicist George Gamow, Einstein had to admit that his addition of a factor (a "cosmological constant" that he designated by the Greek letter *Lamda*) into his own mathematical formulas to explain what he had assumed to the essential sameness of the universe, had been the greatest blunder of his career.[16]

As might be expected, there has been a great deal of criticism of this "anthropic" argument, the most predictable being that the only real reason it can be made is that we humans happen to be here to make this self-congratulatory observation. Might not the inhabitants of any other inhabitable planet elsewhere in the universe also say the same in respect to themselves? If so, this, in turn, would only seem to prove the authors' point — although they might have to change the "anthropic" part of their title with a new term suggesting various other forms of intelligent life.

Instead, probably the only effective way of trying to discredit the Anthropic Principle argument for a Designer of the universe is to speculate that our Universe (we'll capitalize

Einstein and the Image of God

it here since it is the only one we know of for sure) is just one of many other "universes" or perhaps a branch of a gigantic "multiverse" or maybe is just the product of an accidental burp or hiccup from a "quantum vacuum", or of the mysterious "dark energy" mentioned earlier. Krauss thinks that the quantum vacuum explanation is the best one, at least to justify the title of his book, since it seems that a vacuum is the closest to nothing that a physicist can think of. But even he is forced to admit, towards the end, in Chapter 9 of his book, that, when you really get down to it, this "Nothing is Something." Nevertheless, apparently to further refute any anthropic principle argument, Krauss endorses the idea that the laws of physics are just as arbitrary as the number of universes.

In this, Krauss seems to be following the latest ideas of the famed theoretical physicist Steven Hawking. Yet Hawking, who after hinting in the very last sentence of his best selling 1988 book, *A Brief History of Time*, that we are finally getting close to Einstein's goal of understanding "the mind of God," more recently, in his 2010 book, *The Grand Design*, has decided that the latest variety of string theory that he and his colleagues are calling "M-theory" explains everything — although he admits that no one knows for sure really what the "M" in M-Theory stands for. According to Hawking, "it may be 'master', 'miracle', or 'mystery'." Nevertheless, he is sure that "it has eleven space-time dimensions, not ten" and that it allows for virtually an infinite number of universes — maybe as many as 10 followed by 500 zeroes, "each with its own set of laws."[17]

Curiously, it might be noted that until the Anthropic Cosmological Principle was presented by Barrow and Tipler in 1988, there seems to have been no serious thought about

Science and the God of Reason

other or "parallel universes" except in occasional literary fantasies or in the kind of science fiction authored by writers such as Isaac Asimov. Quite the contrary, the philosopher and psychologist William James singled out belief in another universe, in his famous 1896 lecture on "The Will to Believe" as a form of religious escapism; or in his 1904-5 series of lectures on pragmatism, contrasting it to the kind of more absolutistic philosophy produced by "the mind that makes our universe by thinking it, [and which] might, for aught they show us to the contrary, have made any one of a million other universes just as well as this."[18] James then went on to compare such purely speculative philosophy to some forms of religious belief.

Instead, as we shall see in the following section, if one wishes to really try to serve an indictment and try God in a way that discredits any belief in him, there are much more serious charges to be made than by summoning imaginary universes that no one has ever seen, and which, given the laws of physics that we're stuck with, still remain impossible to detect.

C: God and the Problem of Evil

If you were to wager on what might be the single-most reason why people are inclined to reject the whole idea of God — other than the fact that the idea of there being a God tends to be seen as threat to our personal independence — you would be wise to place your bet not on theoretical physics or on any other supposedly scientific arguments against God, but on the hard facts of evil and suffering. Thus, the Nobel Prize-winning physicist Richard Feynman, when he was asked on TV why he was an atheist, had only one simple answer: "…

Einstein and the Image of God

how do you answer the 'where's God' question in the face of atrocities like the Holocaust?"[19]

This also was Einstein's biggest problem when, although he insisted that he believed in God, he had to face the same question. When asked about such monumental suffering back in 1915, apparently in reference to the great slaughters already starting to take place on the battlefields of World War I, Einstein replied:

> I see with only deep regret that God punishes his children for their numerous stupidities, for which only he can be held responsible. In my opinion, only his nonexistence could excuse him.[20]

Predictably, some have used this quotation to try to assert that Einstein really was an atheist, despite his denials that he was. However, as we have already seen, Einstein believed that his solution to this problem was the same as Spinoza's — not to deny that there is a God, but to instead to hold a view of God that is so deterministic that Einstein denied that we really are free, or at most, only free enough to regret the evils that we had no choice but to do. In other words, Einstein, according to his theories about evil, had to hold God to be responsible. Yet, if we can believe what he said in some of his letters, rather than blame God, Einstein definitely blamed the German people for their having allowed Hitler to come to power and held them to be guilty of the crimes the Nazis committed.[21]

The problem is hardly new. As far back as seventeen centuries ago, St. Augustine stated the problem rather succinctly: "Either God cannot abolish evil or He will not: if He cannot, He is not all powerful: if He will not, He is not all

Science and the God of Reason

good." But Augustine was only paraphrasing the same dilemma — in terms of a single God rather than many gods — as noted by the philosopher, Epicurus, centuries before. And then of course, there is the biblical Book of Job, with its questioning of God's goodness and justice.

Faced with this same dilemma, the Holocaust survivor, Elie Weisel, who was not lucky to have been safely in the USA like Einstein or Feynman when the Holocaust was taking place, wrote in *Night*, his 1972 autobiographical account of his ordeal, that although he never once doubted that there is a God, he did begin to doubt God's power, and, after his horrifying experience in Auschwitz, he began, nor had he since ceased, to doubt that God is good.

But should God necessarily be understood as being all-good? The Hebrew Scriptures do not seem to uniformly describe God that way. And although the New Testament, especially the Gospels, generally give the impression of God as a loving "Father," some of the parables that Jesus used demonstrate that at times this loving care (as noted earlier) can be a "tough love" that punishes when correction is called for. And while correction or punishment may have a good or legitimate role to play in the overall scheme of things, we don't generally think of it as something to look forward to or find to be desirable. Hence we probably shouldn't be surprised when, if we take another look at Webster's definition of God with its description of God as "eternal, infinite, all-powerful, and all-knowing," we should especially note that it does *not* include "all-good" or "all-loving." The only hint of all-goodness appears in the definition of God in the *Oxford Dictionary of the English Language*, where in addition to a shorter description of God in terms similar to Webster's

Einstein and the Image of God

definition, we find added "[the] source of all moral authority."

While this additional note, which might possibly reflect one of the arguments presented in favor of belief in God that was especially favored by C. S. Lewis — who for most of his life taught at Oxford — it does little to explain the real problem of evil that most people find so perplexing. The problem is not the evils that afflict people who bring them on themselves or who perhaps deserve punishment. Instead, the problem is the evils that afflict the innocent, the floods, earthquakes, the storms, typhoons, fires, and all the other so-called (by the insurance industry) "Acts of God" that destroy the lives of countless persons who seem to have in no way deserved such suffering. How excuse a supposedly good God for such injustice?

This is the age-old problem that, due to the classic study written by philosopher Gottfried Wilhelm Leibniz (1646-1716), is called *Theodicy* — meaning "God's Justice." According to Leibniz, despite all the evils that afflict us, God created "the best possible" world, and that no matter how bad these evils may seem, they are ultimately for our own betterment. Four years after the 1755 Lisbon earthquake which killed many thousands of — some have even claimed up to 100,000 — people, Leibniz's view was ridiculed by the skeptic Voltaire in his satirical novel *Candide*, where the lovable but gullible character, after whom the book is named, is assured by a "Professor Pangloss" (Prof. All-Words) that every day in every way the world is getting better and better.

However, Oxford's C. S. Lewis probably put it much more accurately in his book on *The Problem of Pain*, where he changed just one word in Leibniz's famous saying. As Lewis saw it, God created "the *only* possible world"! In other words,

Science and the God of Reason

if God was going to create at all, God is stuck with the kind of world we have.

Such a view, of course, severely limits the view of God as omnipotent or almighty. It's not that God couldn't make a different world at all, but if we assume that what God wanted is a world filled with free creatures, and not just preprogrammed robots, it is a world where all kinds of things can happen — ranging from the random behavior described by quantum mechanics to the exercise of free will by creatures like us who can love or hate, cooperate with or, unfortunately, make life miserable for others. In other words, it is the world as described by the theory of evolution, not just in the biological realm, but on a universal scale, much as described by physicist Eric Chaisson in his 2001 book on *Cosmic Evolution*, or by the British physicist and clergyman John Polkinghorne in his little collection of talks which he titled *Chaos, Quarks, and Christianity*.

But we need to be more precise about this matter of human freedom and its relationship to the problem of evil, which, as we've already seen, caused Einstein to end up contradicting himself. It should be clear by now that in a world where a kind of quantum randomness appears to be characteristic of the very foundation of physics, the connection between evil and freedom works in both directions. Free creatures can and often do will to commit outright evils. But at the same time, when understood as the result of an evolutionary process, freedom could not exist except in a world where randomness or chance is part of that same process. And this is a process in which a lot of accidents occur, such as earthquakes, floods, and other so-called "Acts of God" that cause so much suffering. If, as Darwin said, evolution comes about as a result of natural selection, it is a selection made between random variations, some of which will prove advantageous, while others will prove disastrous. Meanwhile, survival of the fittest implies the perishing of the unfit.

Furthermore, it is a world where the true exercise of free will becomes possible not just when we have a choice between various options, but only when our intelligence succeeds in being aware of and mastering the unintelligent and often random forces that too often drive us to make poor or even stupid choices. In other words, until we achieve this level of *reflective* thought — not just knowing or perceiving something, but as Teilhard de Chardin termed it, "knowing that we know"— thanks to the evolution of the human brain and using it intelligently, we may only be making random choices, not exercising genuine freedom.

As we will see in the next chapter, this progression from a clocklike universe to one in which humans can enjoy and bear the responsibility of freedom is something that Spinoza finally figured out and what made it possible for him to title the summary of his world-view as being *Ethics* rather than, let's say, "physics" or "mechanics." Unfortunately, this basic randomness of the quantum universe — something that Einstein found it difficult to accept, even though his own theories had led others to this conclusion — seems to have prevented Einstein from accepting Spinoza's final viewpoint on this matter. This was especially unfortunate, considering how important Spinoza's basic insights were to be in the centuries that were to follow him.

Conclusion

In this chapter's survey of the three major problems that atheists have with the philosophical or reasoned arguments

Science and the God of Reason

for believing that there is a God, we have seen that, at least in the first two cases — God's "existence" and proposed reasons to see God's "hand" or "mind" in some way involved in the way the universe appears to be designed — those who resist or deny these arguments end up having to propose alternative beliefs of their own. For if to *believe* means to hold, usually with some strength, an opinion that lacks any overwhelming proof, then surely to hold that the existence of the universe and its intricate working is all a mere accident, is as much a "belief" or perhaps even requires more faith than believing that it is, as Einstein repeatedly claimed, the work of "an infinitely superior intelligence." The same probably goes for the belief that science will eventually turn up evidence of other "universes" or a "multiverse," especially given that the speed of light effectively limits our ability to gather further scientific information. Any claims made beyond that are likely to remain, as physicist Eric Chaisson has said, not science but "science fiction."[22]

However, when it comes to the problem of evil, science, especially evolutionary theory, turns out to be much more of an asset than an obstacle to religious faith. Not that it proves that there is a God, but in a way it lets God "off the hook" so to speak, unless we are to blame God for having created a universe at all. But if God is love, in the sense of self-giving, did God have any choice other than to create?

At this point, no doubt, traditional believers will no doubt be puzzled. What about angels? Did they evolve? And the ones that revolted: did they not have free will? But these are the kind of problems that perhaps will have to be dealt with in the second part of this book, problems concerning the world-views held by writers in past millennia — some of which (to

Einstein and the Image of God

be more specific), like belief in angels, were most likely not even part of the biblical world-view to begin with.

Meanwhile, since we have gotten back to a kind of basic philosophical belief in the form of the kind of rationalized "deism" as well as a new approach to the problem of evil which Einstein found so vexing, it is time to turn, in the next chapter to the "New Deism" that atheist Victor Stenger, who out-published all the other "new atheists" during his long lifetime, found so puzzling. We will begin with Spinoza, whose own peculiar variety of deism no one, including even Einstein, seems to have fully understood.

---

[1] James, William, *Varieties of Religious Experience*, 182.
[2] Ibid., 184.
[3] Ibid., 185.
[4] *L'Oservatore Romano*, April 12, 2006.
[5] In Hebrew *tohu w'bohu*, literally "trackless waste and emptiness," or as more commonly translated "a formless void."
[6] Plato, *Timaeus*, 51a.
[7] 2 Macc 7:28, NRSV translation. The Greek reads, *'hoti ouk ex ontōn*, i.e., "out of things that were not."
[8] Metaxas, *Wall Street Journal*, 12/26/2014.
[9] Krauss, Lawrence, *A Universe from Nothing*, 26, 34-35, 77. The expression "flat universe" apparently refers to graphic depictions of the expansion rate of the universe. A gradually descending line would represent universe in the state of collapse, while a sharply ascending line would represent an accelerating universe in a state of explosive disintegration. (See graph on p.81 of Krauss' book.)
[10] www.whillyard.com/science-pages/steinhardt-turok.html (accessed 5/29/2015).
[11] For the latest discussion regarding the implications of these discoveries, see http://hubpages.com/education/Different-Models-of-the-

Science and the God of Reason

Universe-That-Revise-the-Big-Bang-Theory (Accessed 3/19/2016).

[12] From the Latin preposition *ex* ("from") and the verb *sistere* ("to place," "to cause," or "to stand").

[13] Hart, David Bentley. *The Experience of God*, 106-08.

[14] Wallace, Stanley. *Does God Exist? The Craig-Flew Debate*, 204. It should be noted that in this same debate, Craig argued that if the Universe did begin thirteen some billion years ago, this would indicate that it would seem to be the result of a decision, otherwise it would have always existed; hence an argument for a person-like God.

[15] Flew, Anthony. *There Is a God*, 75, 123-26.

[16] Isaacson, Walter. *Einstein: Life and Universe*, 356, 613 n.55.

[17] Hawking and Mlodinow, *The Grand Design*, 117-8.

[18] James, William, *Collected Works*, Lecture 1: "The Present Dilemma in Philosophy."

[19] www.latimesblog.lastimes.com/jacketcopy/2010/09/herman-wouk-richard-feynman-science-and-religion.html (accessed 12/5/2014)

[20] Calaprice, 231.

[21] Ibid.,164-69

[22] Chaisson, Eric, *Cosmic Evolution*, 9.

Einstein and the Image of God

Chapter 3
The New Deism

In several of the later of his many books promoting atheism, Victor J. Stenger evidenced some interest in what he called "the New Deism."[1] It would apparently be a kind of deism in which the basic laws of nature allow for more flexibility than in the Enlightenment version which was largely formulated in terms of a clock-work, Newtonian-type universe.

We already have had a glimpse of its predecessor in Spinoza, who was one of the first and perhaps the most innovative articulator of what was soon to be described as "Deism"— a strictly rational belief in a single God who designed and created the universe, but who is neither involved with the universe nor particularly involved with human affairs. However, in Spinoza's version, to begin with, God appears to be completely in control of everything, to the point where if anything goes wrong, God is ultimately to blame.

The roots of deism go much further back than Spinoza, probably to the very beginnings of philosophy, which much like the later deism, evidenced an attempt to justify belief in a single God or origin of the universe. This effort was apart from or even in opposition to what was, back then, the popular beliefs in many gods, with each one of them in charge of a particular people or even within a single nation, different departments of life. In contrast to these ancient beliefs, Plato's and Aristotle's ideas of God, largely based on reason or strictly logical thinking, could be described as being "deist."

Unlike the deism of ancient times, the deism of the Seventeenth Century Enlightenment and the following centuries was basically spawned by two simultaneous

Einstein and the Image of God

revolutions, followed by a third upheaval, which was largely political. The first of these revolutions was that movement in European life known as "Humanism," which laid great stress on both going back to the original sources of Western culture, not only those found in Greek and Roman learning, but even reexamining the origins of Western religion, beginning with a demand for more accurate and reliable copies of the Sacred Scriptures in their original languages. All this, in turn, partly in concert with the invention of the printing press, led to the Protestant Reformation.

The second revolution was a scientific one. It began with Copernicus' heliocentric theory, founded on the basis of mathematical calculations that led to the conclusion that the Sun, and not, as had always been assumed, the Earth, is the center of our solar system, which even then, was considered the center of the whole Universe. This theory was confirmed, less that a century later, by Galileo who, claimed to have shown, by means of the newly invented telescope, that what Copernicus had proposed as a theory or hypothesis must now be accepted as a proven fact. And it was in 1632, the same year that Galileo was summoned to explain himself to the Roman Inquisition, that Spinoza was born.

The third revolution was a political or social one, indeed a series of them that included a religious revolt in England led by the fanatical Puritan, Oliver Cromwell. This was followed a century or so later by the American Revolution. All this reached a culmination in the French Revolution that overthrew the monarchy and the established Church, and its claims to "revealed" truth along with it.

Accordingly, while Spinoza's seemingly pantheistic God may appear to be the inverse of the distant and aloof God of 17th century deism, in reality the motives that led to those views were very similar. Thus what we have known as deism

The New Deism

today, as well as Spinoza's radical views, were mostly associated with rationalism, reliance on scientific discovery, and the rejection of organized religion — particularly any religion that claimed to depend on divine revelation. While the epicenter of this movement was undoubtedly in France, this strictly philosophical approach to religion spread rapidly, especially westward, not just to Great Britain, but even across the Atlantic to the English colonies in America. In fact, a notable number of the founding fathers of the United States were deists, even if they still went through the motions of attending their various Christian churches. Most prominent among these, especially as a deist, was Thomas Jefferson, who even went to the trouble of preparing his own version of the gospels, in which all mention of any supernatural or miraculous events were carefully removed, with Jesus reduced to being an inspiring teacher of morality.

The new deism which Stenger referred to, however, seems to span a wider range of thought than what Jefferson and his free-thinking colleagues had in mind. One form is a revival of nature pantheism, with its emphasis on nature or *everything* being part of God. Another form might be a "monistic pantheism," with its emphasis on *God* being everything, of which Spinoza was accused. Finally, in this chapter, we will be looking at still another variation of the same association of God and the natural world, called *panentheism*, with its addition of the *en* (the Greek for "in") — thus literally meaning "everything [being] *in* God" or conversely, God being *in* everything, and its development from the thought of the evolutionary philosopher Alfred North Whitehead.

However, because Spinoza has been credited with introducing this line of thought into more recent Western philosophy, it is probably now the time to take a more detailed look at exactly what Spinoza was saying before we venture into the evolutionary "Process Theology" developed by the followers of Whitehead, or the development of an evolutionary interpretation of Christianity that will be taken up later as part of Chapter 6 (in Part II) of this book.

A: God in Spinoza's Thought

Spinoza had much to say regarding organized religion that outraged his contemporaries, especially in his *Tractatus theologico-politicus* which he had first published in 1670, seven years before his death. But even by then, his views regarding the relationship between God and the natural world seem to have been misunderstood. As he wrote to Henry (Heinrich) Oldenburg, a former German diplomat who, after settling in London, had become the first Secretary of the Royal Society:

> I recognize that I have a very different idea of God than what the modern Christians make of him. And I regard God as the principle and cause of all things, immanent and not passing.[2]

But then, to clarify and further defend this view, especially God's immanent presence in nature, Spinoza quoted the New Testament, where St. Luke depicts St. Paul in *The Acts of the Apostles* as quoting from an ancient Greek poet who wrote "In him [God] we have our life, our movement, and our being." [3]

Furthermore, in a later letter to Oldenburg, Spinoza complained that:

> ... as to the view of certain people that I identify god with nature (taken as a kind of mass or corporal nature), they are quite mistaken.[4]

The New Deism

Although both of these remarks are important, the last one is especially crucial for an accurate understanding of what Spinoza was getting at, for in his posthumously published *Ethics*, critics have almost always have focused entirely on Spinoza's expression *Deus sive Natura*, which is usually translated as "God or Nature," but which he actually used only three or four times in the concluding Part V. Yet from this they deduce that in Spinoza's mind, God and Nature must have been one and the same. And this they insist upon, despite the fact that Spinoza mentioned God over five-hundred times in this same book, without using the word nature and nearly eighty-some times discussing God's own nature or else God's relationship with the natural world, but without using the *Deus sive Natura* phrase. So why did Spinoza use that seemingly loaded phrase at all?

The first reason seems to be to stress God's close relationship to the natural world, what Jefferson called (in the Declaration of Independence) "Nature's God." The second reason was to stress how God's nature is reflected in the natural world, that the latter is a mirror image, as it were of the former, with God's nature described as *natura naturans* (God as determining the nature of things) and Nature's nature as *natura naturata* (nature as determined by God). This important distinction can be found in the first paragraph of the long "Note" attached to Proposition XXIX. This distinction and the language used to describe it, was really nothing new. In fact, it can be found in the book *Periphysion* ("About Nature") of John Scotus Eriugena, the 9th century Irish philosopher-theologian.

As a final detail regarding the *Deus sive Natura* issue regarding Spinoza, we might add that the Latin word *sive* does not mean exactly the same as the more usual Latin word for "or," which is *vel*, and implies equivalence or the same

Einstein and the Image of God

thing under a different name. Instead, *sive* or *seu* (another spelling) implies an alternative explanation for the same phenomenon, but not a simple identification of the two explanations. However, to understand this point better, we have to go back to Part I of Spinoza's *Ethics* and his understanding or definition of God to begin with, this followed by a further explanation.

> By God, I mean a being absolutely infinite — that is, a substance consisting of infinite attributes, of which each expresses eternal and infinite essentiality.
>
> Explanation — I say absolutely infinite, not infinite after its kind: for of a thing infinite only after its kind, infinite attributes may be denied; but that which is absolutely infinite, contains in its essence whatever expresses reality, and involves no negation.[5]

But here we are again faced with the issue of what Spinoza meant by the word *substance,* which takes us back again to his complaint shared with Oldenburg about people thinking that he was talking about "a kind of mass or corporal nature" in the parenthetical clause in the last quoted letter. Thus, in his *Ethics,* Spinoza was careful to state that:

> By substance, I mean that which is in itself, and which is conceived through itself: in other words, that of which a conception can be formed independently of any other conception.[6]

Or to put Spinoza's point in less conceptual and more literal terms, a *substance* is, as was pointed out toward the end of Chapter 1, that which "stands under" or underpins a more visible or perceptible reality: thus by the word "God"

The New Deism

Spinoza understood that Being or unseen reality on which the existence of everything else depends.

Given this hidden nature of God, how then can we know anything about him? Spinoza's answer is that among the infinite number of divine attributes, there are especially two that we humans can perceive. These are *thought* and *extension*. These two attributes of God are first mentioned in a corollary or additional point that follows Proposition XIV in the *Ethics* which states: "Besides God, no substance can be granted or conceived." Therefore, as the corollary states: "It follows ... that extension and thought are either attributes of God or ... accidents (*affectiones*) of the attributes of God."[7] These attributes are perceptible to us in the order or design of nature that our minds perceive, as well in the concrete qualities, especially in the vastness and the beauty of nature that we see around us.

Given this doctrine of the two extensions of God which we can perceive both in ourselves and in nature, it is easy to see why most people, including theologians of Spinoza's time, considered him to be, if not an atheist, then, instead, a pantheist — which to their eyes, amounted almost to the same thing. After all, they reasoned, if *everything* is an extension of God, then *nothing* in particular is God, least of all in the biblical understanding of the divinity.

Thus, it is easy to see why Einstein, who claimed that he believed in Spinoza's God, saw God, especially God's *thought*, expressed in the laws of nature and said "I want to know God's thoughts; the rest are details"[8], and repeatedly told friends and other inquirers that it was his ambition to know even more fully what God thinks. But, when it comes to Spinoza's assertion that God is revealed in his attribute of extension, Einstein was not so sure about that, avowing that "I don't think I can call myself a pantheist."[9]

Einstein and the Image of God

However, before we leave the subject of Spinoza, we need to look more closely at the moral or ethical determinism that Einstein admitted gave him so much comfort and which he believed that he found in Spinoza's thought. Most likely Einstein found it in the passage in Part I of the *Ethics* that says that:

> Nothing in the universe is contingent, but all things are conditioned to exist and operate in a particular manner by the necessity of the divine nature.[10]

Not only that, this assertion is followed by others that appear to assert that both the human intellect and will, acting together, can only comprehend and carry out what it perceives as modifications of the attributes of God, but that even these modifications are themselves dictated in such a way by divine nature that they "...could not have been brought into being by God in any manner or in any order different from that which has in fact obtained."[11]

At this point in this short survey of Spinoza's thought, we could be tempted to show how, in the succeeding four parts of his *Ethics*, Spinoza appears to have gradually softened or modified his views on this matter, particularly when it comes to the question of human freedom. Perhaps this was a result of his own struggles to defend his views against mounting opposition, as evidenced in his letters to Oldenburg, as well as perhaps his exposure to the views of some Mennonite Christian friends, whose church he occasionally attended and whose beliefs were in opposition the views of divine predestination taught by Dutch Calvinism.[12]

Accordingly, especially in Part V of his *Ethics*, Spinoza described the process by which humans can gradually learn to overcome their emotions by understanding them and thus the beginning of what we like to think is a certain degree of human freedom. Perhaps, had it not been for his rather early death, just short of forty-five years of age, he would have further refined these ideas. However, for the purposes of this chapter, which is to introduce a new kind of thinking about God, this summary of Spinoza's radical views will have to have served its purpose. It is now time to move on to an even more radical revision of ideas, not just about God, but regarding the nature of everything.

B: *Reality in Process*

Alfred North Whitehead, born in Great Britain in 1861, first gained public notice when he and his former pupil at Cambridge University, Bertrand Russell, jointly published a ground-breaking three volume book, which in imitation of Newton's famous work, was brashly titled *Principia Mathematica*. After that, Whitehead turned from mathematics more to the philosophy of science, and then to philosophy in general — especially when he was persuaded to cross over to America in 1924 to teach philosophy at Harvard University. Having been born only two years after the publication of Darwin's revolutionary ideas, Whitehead's thought could not avoid confronting, and to some extent even absorbing, the whole concept of evolution.

However, Whitehead's acceptance and use of the theory of evolution was not applied simply to biological science, but rather to *all* of reality. Thus everything and every one, including God, are seen in terms of "process." All this was fully explained by Whitehead in his Gifford Lectures which he was invited to give in Edinburgh and that were first published in 1929 under the title *Process and Reality: An Essay in Cosmology*. But this immensely important work is hardly an "essay" in the sense we use that word today. Instead, it is an

Einstein and the Image of God

immense, and exhaustively detailed, venture into a whole new way of thinking of everything in the universe, which to Whitehead's way of thinking, even includes God.

As result, among the more theologically-inclined of his former pupils in America (where Whitehead died in 1947) and his followers elsewhere, there has sprung up a school of what is called "Process Theology." It is they who coined the term, *panentheism*, to express their view of everything being contained *in* God, much the same, as we have already seen, when Spinoza quoted that passage from the Acts of the Apostles about our living, moving, and being in God. So although the term "panentheism" (again with a stress on the additional *"en"*) is relatively new, the idea is seen by some as having roots in Plato's thought. Interestingly, Whitehead, it seems, considered himself to be basically a Platonist. This should not be a surprise considering his early interest with mathematics and Plato's early training in the Pythagorean school.[13] Hence we should not be surprised to find the same idea expressed by Plotinus, the Neo-Platonist philosopher who insisted that "God is not just everywhere...God is the everywhere in which everything has its existence." [14]

Accordingly, in the final chapter of his great masterwork, Whitehead had spoken of an "antecedent" or "primeval" nature of God, from which the universe takes it origin, but also a "consequent nature" of God within whom all individual beings or entities (usually called "occasions" in Whitehead's evolutionary vocabulary) find their fulfillment, as well as contribute to God's own fulfillment. The theological movement to develop the further implications of Whitehead's thought along more explicitly Christian lines seems to have stemmed mostly from the work of his one-time teaching assistant at Harvard, Charles Hartshorne. From these beginnings, the movement has flourished, particularly in

The New Deism

Whitehead's adopted home, even if only recently, his thought — especially in its theological implications — has begun taking root in his land of origin.

Given Whitehead's early background in mathematical abstractions, it is no wonder that this great philosophical masterwork, especially in its initial chapters, appears to be almost impenetrable. For example, the second chapter of Part I ("The Speculative Scheme"), presents a "categoreal scheme" that consists of eight categories of existence and twenty-seven categories of explanation, the ninth of which asserts (here I quote, word for word):

> That *how* an actual entity *becomes* constitutes *what* that actual entity *is*; so that the two descriptions of an actual entity are not independent. Its 'being' is constituted by its 'becoming.' This is the 'principle of process.' [15]

The above passage, with its equation of being with becoming, or even the replacement of the former by the latter as the chief object of our attention, is of paramount importance if we are to understand Whitehead's concept of God. For as he said in another place in the final section of his extended treatise, "...God is not to be treated as an exception to all metaphysical principles, invoked to save their collapse." Instead, "He [God] is their chief exemplification."[16] Thus God's being, seen as a constituent of the entire cosmos, is in a state of eternal becoming. So while Whitehead admitted that, conceptually-speaking, "God and the World stand over against each other... " a sentence or so later he also insisted that "no two actualities [i.e., God and the World] can be torn apart: each is all in all."[17] If so, then the traditional transcendentalist understanding of theism, that is to say, God as "totally other," is radically undercut.

Einstein and the Image of God

Also undercut, in this rethinking of reality, is the rigid determinism that seemed to follow from Spinoza's view of God's nature and which, despite Spinoza's attempts to soften its consequences, eventually gave Einstein so much trouble. One result was that Einstein found it almost impossible to fit quantum mechanics, which his own discoveries regarding the photoelectric theory of light as "quanta" or packets of energy had given rise to — winning him a Nobel Prize in 1922 — into his own mental map, declaring that he refused to believe that God "plays dice."[18] To the contrary, according to Joseph A. Bracken[19], Whitehead's view of reality in process almost seems made-to-order for a view of the physical world born from a sea of energy in the state of quantum flux.[20]

Whitehead also wrote of God as being, as it were, "the lure for feeling, the eternal urge of desire,"[21] a source of endless "creativity"[22] and of "innovation" or "novelty."[23] Most noteworthy, however, is Whitehead's distinction between God's antecedent or "primordial" nature and God's "consequent nature." The former is "God in abstraction, alone with himself."[24] On the other hand "The consequent nature of God is conscious; and it is the realization of the actual world in the unity of his nature, and through the transformation of his wisdom."[25] It is between these two poles, during the eons of evolution, both past and what is yet to come, in which "The perfection of God's subjective aim, derived from the completeness of his primordial nature, issues into the character of his consequent nature."[26] Even if "the revolts of destructive evil" are taken into regard, yet "the image — and it is but an image — the image under which this operative growth of God's nature is best conceived, is that of a tender care that nothing be lost."[27] Thus God is seen as "the great companion — the fellow sufferer who understands."[28]

The New Deism

The question remains, however, whether this radical modification of theism is any longer compatible with the "unmoved mover" concept of God derived from Aristotle. Apparently Whitehead believed that it was not, and that it was this Greek philosophical understanding of divinity, foreign to the more dynamic Hebrew concept of God, combined with the notion of the "eminently real" (that is, a static concept of *being* rather than *becoming*), that has "infused tragedy into the histories of Christianity and Mahometanism."[29] All this, Whitehead believed, ill-accords with "the brief Galilean vision of humility" which "dwells upon the tender elements in the world, which slowly and in quietness operate by love; and it finds purpose in the present immediacy of a kingdom not of this world."[30]

Curiously, none of the "new atheists" seem to have seriously investigated, or even to be aware of, contemporary panentheistic thought. No doubt this is partly due to the difficulties in following all the intricate turns of thought in Whitehead's great masterwork.[31] Nor does Whitehead's concept of God present the easy target for critics of the kind of theism found in more traditional Christian thought, especially that shared with the other biblically based religions. Finally, due to the relatively low-key and liberally humanistic picture of Jesus presented by Whitehead and most of his followers, the new atheists, if they were to pay any attention to the process theologians at all, are inclined to classify them, like Stenger did, among the "new deists."

Given this situation, what can be done to rescue this more dynamic panentheistic concept of the divine from oblivion?

C: A Non-theistic Christianity?

This last question takes us to where perhaps John Shelby Spong, the retired American Episcopalian bishop, whose ideas

Einstein and the Image of God

about the Trinity we've already seen, fits in, particularly in his efforts to promote what he calls a "non-theistic" Christianity, a Christianity that, as much as possible, avoids thinking of God as a person and instead focuses its attention on Jesus.

Spong's 2007 book, *Jesus for the Non-religious*, follows a line of thought that he has been developing over many years — inspired by the call of the German theologian Deitrich Bonhöffer for a "religionless Christianity," one that embraces all of reality rather than, as has most religions in the past, served as an escape-hatch from it. Basing his reasoning on that of his theological mentors, Paul Tillich, and the Anglican bishop J. A. T. Robinson — Spong really does seem to think that such a non-theistic Christianity is possible. For this, Spong earned the notice of Daniel Dennett[32], but also the distain of Richard Dawkins[33], and the outrage of many traditional Episcopalians.

Beginning in Part 3 of his 2007 book, Spong summed up our evolutionary history not only in both cosmic and biological terms, but also psychologically in regard to the development of religion, beginning with primitive animism — the belief that everything, not just living beings, but even the earth, water, and the sky have a "soul" which inhabits them. Spong sees this latter development as motivated by both fear (primarily fear of death) and a longing for security. However, instead of the fear-driven and guilt-filled religion that had developed down through the ages, Spong would offer us a non-theistic liberation from all that has gone before by proposing that we shift our attention to a view centered on the humanity of Jesus. This is because, as Spong wrote:

> ... in the fullness of Jesus' humanity we can experience what it means to live beyond the barriers of our evolutionary past and soar into a humanity that is spirit-filled, open to the source of

The New Deism

life and love and what Paul Tillich called, as his name for God, the 'ground of being'.[34]

Or again, much as the subtitle of his 1974 book (*Christpower: Recovering the Divine at the Heart of the Human*) indicated, Jesus "becomes for us the doorway into what human beings mean by the word 'divinity'."[35]

To accomplish this same goal, Spong began (in Part 1 of this newer book) by invoking what he considers to be the latest New Testament interpretation, primarily the output of the "Jesus Seminar"[36] — ignoring the devastating criticisms of the eminent New Testament exegete and historian of the first century (and recently retired Anglican bishop) N. Thomas Wright.[37] Nevertheless, following the path marked out by Rudolph Bultmann, Spong developed a plan for a "demythologized" Christianity with no virgin birth, no miracles, no resurrection — at least not to be understood literally. It is also an approach which, it almost goes without saying, departs nearly entirely from the long history of the development of Christian doctrine concerning the divine identity of Christ. This history has been traced in great detail by such authorities as Aloys Grillmeier, or more recently, summarized on a more popular level, as well as in a much more skeptical tone, by Richard Rubenstein, who concentrates on the politics of the fourth century, and still more recently, in terms of first century developments within the New Testament, by Bart Ehrman.

Without necessarily adopting all of Spong's views regarding his interpretations of the gospels, or even adopting his "non-theistic" terminology, I would suggest that what Spong has attempted to do points us in the direction that Christianity, and with it theism — despite Spong's rhetoric — may have to go if it really does wish to survive and to continue to provide a convincing vision of ultimate reality and source of ultimate meaning. The same might be said regarding Daniel Maguire's more recent, and even more radically strident, proposal that we strive to create a "Christianity without God."

However, at this point it might be opportune to point out again that theism as we have known it has been generally predicated as if the idea of God as a "person" is to be taken literally, as if it were not merely a symbolic objectification or projection of human religious experience or even of philosophical theorization. But to say that we experience God as "personal" or analogously ascribe person-like characteristics to the ultimate and still largely unknown ground of being is not to say that God is a person in any usual or ordinary sense of the contemporary meaning of that word.

This same confusion of a symbol with its referent seems to have also motivated theologian Karl Rahner's suggestion that we declare a moratorium on the use of that same word when it comes to Christian expositions of God as a "Trinity."[38] Nevertheless, it should be noticed that these various attempts, as it were, to "de-personalize" God, be they Spong's call for a "non-theistic Christianity" or Einstein's appeal to a more "Cosmic Religion," are all predicated on the inadequacy of our traditional personifications. It would seem that our traditional analogies have suffered more from a lack rather than an excess of imagination. If so, then we need to keep this same lesson very much in mind as we explore the other alternatives.

Conclusion

In this chapter we have explored only three variations of the proposed substitutes for the kind of theism or picture of God

The New Deism

that has long been associated with the Bible, particularly the Hebrew Scriptures found in what Christians call the Old Testament. It is also the same picture adopted by Islam, which in turn, especially in that light of recent events, has redoubled its liability to be rejected, even by those who seek to remain religious.

We saw that one of these proposals, that advanced by Spinoza back in the 17th century, seemed so radical and caused so much confusion (was it a form of pantheism or outright atheism?), that even back then the emerging rationalistic deism of that period largely ignored it or rejected it.

Likewise, we have also seen an equally radical approach proposed by the Twentieth Century philosopher, A. N. Whitehead, which begins with a view of God that in some ways reminds us of Spinoza's starting point. Moreover, due to its evolutionary presuppositions, Whitehead gives us a view of divine and human creativity and freedom that far surpasses Spinoza's rigid systemization. The problem is that Whitehead's intricate schematization and puzzling vocabulary has largely shut off access to his revolutionary thought except through nearly heroic efforts of his devoted followers among the academic specialists known as "Process Philosophers" and "Process Theologians."

This leaves us with what some may view as a last resort, John Shelby Spong's proposal of a "non-theistic Christianity" — one which would abandon theology or such "God-talk" altogether and focus all our attention on Jesus. This sounds fine enough, until one asks how we are to concentrate on what Jesus said and did when it is obvious that his whole life was dedicated to carrying out what he believed was his "Father's" (that is, God's) will and establishing God's rule or "Kingdom" on this earth. How are we to model our lives on Jesus without centering them on the same God on whom he centered his

Einstein and the Image of God

life? Or again, how can we revere Jesus as "the Image of God" if we don't take the reality of God seriously to begin with?

It is this last question and the problem it presents that must concern us, keeping in mind Einstein's earlier warning that the majority of mankind needs a personalized idea or image of the deity on which to focus their ideals and hopes. For as he said, without it they are in danger of loosing a sense of the transcendent or without the possibility of fulfilling their "metaphysical needs."[39]

If Einstein had lived on to see all the more recent developments in the field of cosmology, he would have seen his concept or image of God increasingly turn into a heartless and cold abstraction without compassion for the human race or for whatever other intelligent life that may exist in the universe — or, for that matter, for any other "universes" that might exist. So although he understood mankind's need for a personal God, Einstein would have had us outgrow that need, naïvely believing that humanity can survive without a God who cares. If that is the case, then maybe, in the end, those atheists who claim Einstein as one of their own are right, because what person with human feelings could accept such a God? It is this concern that is the underlying motivation and theme of the next part of this book. In view of all that we know about space and time, we need an image of God, especially now, that is as expansive as the whole Universe.

The New Deism

[1] Stenger 2009a, 234-5; 2009b, 27-28, 97-103, 223-27, 233-6.
[2] Watson, Kirk, trans. *The Good Atheist*, 21st letter.
[3] Acts 17:28; from a poem by Epimenides of Cnossos (6th century BCE).
[4] Spinoza, Elwes trans. *Correspondence* 2009, Letter 73. www.sacred-texts.com/phil/spinoza/corr/corr18/htm (accessed 5/29/2015).
[5] Spinoza, *Ethics*, Part I, Definition VI.
[6] Ibid., Definition III
[7] Ibid., Proposition XIV, Corollary II.
[8] Calaprice, 324.
[9] Jammer, 48
[10] Spinoza, *Ethics*, Proposition XXIX.
[11] Ibid., Propositions XXX-XXXIII.
[12] Watson, Kirk, locations 118, 556.
[13] Cooper, 19
[14] *Enneads*, VI, 8, 16.
[15] Whitehead, A. N., *Process and Reality*, 34-35.
[16] Ibid., 521.
[17] Ibid., 529.
[18] Calaprice, 380, 393.
[19] Bracken, Joseph A. *The World in the Trinity*, Chapter 2.
[20] Whitehead, 176-79; Sherburne, Donald W., *A Key to Whitehead's Process and Reality*, 161-9.
[21] Whitehead, *Process and Reality*, 552.
[22] Ibid., 46-47, 135, 339, 343-44, 522.
[23] Ibid., 31, 135, 249, 529.
[24] Ibid., 50.
[25] Ibid., 524.
[26] Ibidem.
[27] Ibid., 525.
[28] Ibid., 532.
[29] Ibid., 519.
[30] Ibid., 520.
[31] Sherbourne, 2-3.
[32] Dennett, Daniel, *Breaking the Spell*, 2006, 209.

Einstein and the Image of God

[33] Dawkins, Richard, *The God Delusion*, 2008, 269.
[34] Spong, John Shelby, *Jesus for the Non-religious*, 263.
[35] Ibidem.
[36] Funk, Hoover, et al. *The Five Gospels*.
[37] Wright, N. T., 1999b.
[38] Rahner, Karl, 1975, 1208, 1756.
[39] Jammer, 51.

Part II
Christ the Image of God

No one can read the Gospels without feeling the actual presence of Jesus. His personality pulsates with every word. No myth is filled with such life.   *(Albert Einstein)*

Chapter 4
The Historical Jesus

Bishop Spong's call for a "non-theistic Christianity," on the basis of our inability to really know God, or even prove that there is one through philosophical reasoning, may sound very radical. But when we think about it, is it any more radical than the gospel claim that "No one can know the Father except through the Son and those to whom the Son chooses to reveal him"?[1] But then the skeptic will no doubt ask: "Did Jesus really say that?"

In any attempt to discover or even reconstruct a complete picture of the past, we are faced with a basic problem. Can our reconstructions ever capture what *really* happened — especially when the attempt to do so is based on accounts written decades after the subject lived, and which accounts seem to contradict each other in at least some aspects? To answer that general question, this chapter we will be looking at four more specific issues, beginning with what should be the most obvious one, even if only recently it has seemed to become a question at all.

A: Did Jesus Exist?
Surprisingly, the existence of Jesus as a historical fact is not just something that has been questioned more recently, but is something that even Einstein was asked about back in 1929, apparently as a kind of parallel question as to whether or not there is a God to begin with. When asked if he accepted the historical existence of Jesus, Einstein, who had been educated as a child in a Catholic primary school in Munich[2] and who as late as 1929 still claimed that he "often" read the Bible[3] emphatically replied: "Unquestionably! No one can read the

Einstein, and the Image of God

Gospels without feeling the actual presence of Jesus. His personality pulsates in every word. No myth is filled with such life."[4]

This is the question which John Meier, author of the massive five-volume (so far) Anchor Bible study of the historical Jesus began his first volume, published in 1991 with subsequent volumes published in 1994, 2001, 2006 and one scheduled for 2015. Meier has indeed dealt with it in Part I of Volume I of his massive work, especially in four chapters devoted to the *sources* of our knowledge, beginning with the New Testament, then with Josephus (the second century Jewish historian), next, with "Other Pagan and Jewish Sources," and finally with the "*Agrapha*" and apocryphal gospels, such as those discovered at Nag Hammadi in Egypt in 1945. Since Meier's first volume was published, there has been the recent discovery of still another such gospel, which claimed to be by — and even to exonerate — Judas Iscariot! So, if we were to follow Meier and similar historians, the approach seems to amount to the kind of reasoning summed up by the adage "where there is smoke there is fire."

On recent websites devoted to the question "Did Jesus Exist?," we can often find the issue raised in terms of written evidence from Jesus himself, a kind of new twist on Decartes' "I think, therefore I am" — almost as if it was "If you didn't write, you didn't exist." Unfortunately, based on that standard, not even Socrates or Siddartha Gautama (the original Buddha) would have existed either. Everything we know about Jesus and the records of what he was supposed to have taught were only written down by others, who like the disciples of Gautama, claimed to have heard them first hand.

Faced with that fact of history, some other doubters say that in the case of Jesus it is different because people claimed he worked miracles or that he even claimed to be on a par

The Historical Jesus

with God. However, we also know that miracles were claimed — at least by his promoters — to have been worked by Caesar Augustus, and that he himself did not refuse the claim that he was divine. Likewise, the Buddha is said to have walked on water. Despite our disbelief in either type of claim regarding Augustus, or the story about Gautama, does this mean they never existed? Or can our portrayals of the persons involved ever be completely accurate? And even given all this exhaustive research, can anyone claim to be without bias in his or her interpretation? Meier, who is a Roman Catholic, is apparently considered to be unbiased enough to have been selected by the ecumenical board sponsoring the Anchor Bible series. But even the leading title of Meier's study, *A Marginal Jew*, provokes a question, while the subtitle, *Rethinking the Historical Jesus*, promises a somewhat different conclusion than perhaps that which we already have in our minds.

Likewise, this seems to be the case with another set of volumes to which I will most likely refer. It is the pair titled *The Death of the Messiah* by the late and highly respected Catholic scholar Raymond Brown. This work even received praise from a Jewish scholar or two, despite the fact that the title seems to have inferred that Jesus was indeed the long-awaited Messiah. Otherwise, Brown could have decided, or his publisher could have insisted, that the work would be called simply "The Death of Jesus," without using that definitive-sounding word *Messiah* — the title that was to be translated as "Christ."

In any case, separating what actually happened from what people tend to think happened is an unending task. For example, to go back to Meier's remarks about what we mean by the "Historical Jesus," he goes further to distinguish that term from "the historic Jesus," which as he sees it, designates the role that the figure or memory of Jesus has played down through history, even to the present, which will be the topic of the next chapter, but not this one.

B: Levels of Tradition

Granted that Jesus really existed, the next question that probably comes to anyone's mind is to what degree what was written about him can be trusted to give us an accurate record of what actually happened. How much of the gospels is really the "Gospel truth"?

In this regard a very interesting, and no doubt rather surprising, document was published by the Vatican's Pontifical Biblical Commission concerning recommended guidelines for our interpreting and understanding the gospels.[5] Following the basic insights of contemporary scholars, the commission recognized that the texts, which themselves are the products of varied sources, can be classified as belonging to any one of three successive layers of tradition.

At the first and most important level are the actual memories of what Jesus did and said, as passed down from those who claimed to be eye witnesses to the events or direct hearers of his spoken words. Obviously, there can be a wide variety of opinions as to how this first-hand material might be accurately assessed and agreed upon. Meier, for example, believes that among the surest signs that something was actually said, is what biblical scholars call "the criterion of multiple attestation," or in other words, if something is repeated enough times, especially in different gospels, we can be reasonably sure that Jesus actually said or did it. Examples of this would be his baptism in the Jordan, his words over the bread and wine at the Last Supper, his death on the cross, and, as difficult as this may be to accept by some or even many, the claim that he was seen alive again after his death, in other words, his resurrection.

The Historical Jesus

Another sign, championed by Meier and many others, but not all, is "the criterion of discontinuity," which is to say, if Jesus is pictured as saying or doing something that was unusual, perhaps even shocking during his time, you can be reasonably confident that he actually said it. For example, who else would have dared to say that we should "turn the other cheek" or even "love your enemy"? Given these injunctions, it is a criterion that some have a great difficulty in accepting. But on the other hand, if what Jesus is said to have said, like "Love your neighbor as yourself," has been said before, this rouses the suspicion that it was just something the evangelist thought it would be nice to include, even if Jesus hadn't gotten around to actually saying it.

The second level of the tradition is termed the *kerygma*, a term that can be translated as the "message" or "announcement," or "proclamation" — in this case of the good news or *euaggelion*. In general, it can be found in certain often repeated formulas, such as the statement "… and he rose again on the third day, according to the scriptures," which is frequently found in the gospels and epistles, as well as in the earliest creeds. Even Jesus himself is pictured as alluding to that saying when predicting what will happen to him in Jerusalem. The problem here is because it seems to be a stock formula; so again, we might ask if Jesus really did say that?

The third level of the tradition, while it may present the most problems for unsuspecting believers, is the most obvious. It is the material which is often found in only one gospel or if in more than one, it is presented in accounts that seem to flatly contradict what is found, or in some cases, isn't found, in the others. The prime example of this probably is the whole story about Jesus being born of a virgin in Bethlehem.

To begin with, the earliest reference we have to the human origins of Jesus that we have is not from the gospels, but from

Einstein, and the Image of God

St. Paul's letter to the Romans, where we are told that he was "a descendent of David,"[6] and in his letter to the Galatians, where Paul simply describes Jesus as "born of a woman, born a subject of the law."[7] No mention here of a virginal conception or the place of his birth. Next, Mark's gospel, now generally believed to have been the earliest written, says little or nothing about Jesus' origins, except to indicate he was from Nazareth, and had brothers and sisters there. It is only the gospels ascribed to Matthew and Luke that have stories about Mary being a virgin and about she and Joseph journeying down to Bethlehem in Judea and her giving birth to Jesus there.

In these stories, as Raymond Brown pointed out in a little book on *The Birth of the Messiah*, which — almost needless to say — dismayed a lot of conservative Catholics, we have two accounts which diverge rather widely, despite our attempts to lump them together during our Christmas celebrations. Among other discrepancies, we have Matthew introducing wise men journeying from the East and then the Holy Family fleeing to Egypt, while Luke instead has his Holy Family going up peacefully to the temple in Jerusalem to have Jesus properly presented and then returning north, again peacefully, to Nazareth in Galilee. Brown concluded that both stories were made up based on an early tradition, in turn based on Micah's prophecy[8] that indicated that the Messiah, as a descendent of King David, had to come from Bethlehem, the ancestral home town of members of the tribe of Judah. Indeed, a good part of Matthew's story seems to have been put together in a way so as to be able to dredge up quotations from the Hebrew scriptures to apply to the story of Jesus, even if they originally had nothing to do with him, such as Matthew's[9] quote from the Book of Numbers, repeated by the Prophet Hosea, to the effect that "out of Egypt" God had

The Historical Jesus

called "my son" — originally meaning, not Jesus, but God's people, Israel.

Add to these discrepancies Luke's story about Mary visiting her "kinswoman" Elizabeth, who we are told was a member of the tribe of Levi. This would seem to make Mary member of that tribe, leaving us to wonder just how Jesus could really be considered a descendent of David if his biological lineage was clearly that of a Levite! Obviously this whole subject of the particulars of Jesus' birth and early childhood seem to have been specially tailored to suit the intended target audience for whom each of the evangelists had specially in mind. In the case of Matthew, the target audience was a people well-versed in the ancient prophecies, and in the case of Luke, just the opposite, being those for whom Jewish traditions were a whole new world.

Finally, we have the Gospel according to John, probably written many decades later, that backs away from either of the infancy narratives and which seems to take an altogether different approach. Here the presentation of Jesus as God's "Word"[10] is based, it seems, on the Jewish philosopher Philo of Alexandria's adaptation of Stoic ideas of the divine *Logos* in order to translate the Jewish concept of God's Wisdom (*Hochmah/Sophia*) as found in the wisdom books of the Old Testament. Thus, especially here, just as in the case of Matthew's and Luke's stories of Jesus' birth and infancy, we clearly have an example of third level traditions, which, in turn, should seem to give even loyal Catholics considerable leeway in matters of belief.

Although the instruction from the Vatican's Biblical Commission does not carry the weight or doctrinal authority of an official pronouncement regarding matters of faith or morals — one of the four requirements according to the teaching of the First Vatican Council regarding papal infallibility — the fact that it has never been retracted by the Congregation for the Doctrine of the Faith[11] should give us some indication that even in Rome at least some of the churchmen understand that serious questioning of the sources does not mean a rejection of God or of faith in Jesus Christ.

C: The Miracle Stories

Fortunately, the three level approach to the tradition just described also gives us some wiggle-room in confronting another major problem the memory of Jesus poses for many people today, the so-called "miracles," or the to use the word more often used in the gospels, "signs." For many people who admire Jesus as a teacher of morality or an outstanding ethical model for the human race, these miracle stories in the Gospels, which no doubt impressed people in past times, today nevertheless present a barrier to belief or a source of doubt. Did any of these things really happen, or were they all just tales told to enhance his reputation?

Meier devotes 461 pages[12] to the question beginning with an analysis of what "miracles," whether supposed or not, mean or meant to both modern and ancient minds. Meier then goes on, much as other commentators, to distinguish, on the one hand, between "exorcisms," physical healings, raisings from the dead, and other acts involving human psychological and physical health, and on the other hand, what are generally called "nature miracles" — such as walking on water, the multiplication of loaves and fishes, calming storms, etc. The reason for this division of such wonders has generally been to grade them into those that are most explainable in non-miraculous terms. For example, we might explain exorcisms as persuading people that they are cured of what they think of as diabolic possession, or next-in-line, "healing" as addressing and curing psychosomatic symptoms, then raising the dead —

or people who looked like they were dead, especially if they had just recently "died." This leaves the most problematic nature miracles to last place, particularly those that involve things like calming storms, walking on water and multiplying loaves of bread, as being the least believable at all.

Of course, this grading of miracles also underlines why Meier took up the matter of modern vs. ancient minds to begin with. For the mind steeped in modern science and a Newtonian clocklike view of the universe, a lot of this "miracle" talk is hard, if not impossible, to stomach. Like Einstein, when confronted by the quantum physics that his own theory of relativity helped spawn, we refuse to believe that nature may be more "spooky" than we like to think. On the other hand, for the ancients, who apparently saw nature as being extremely fluid, the idea that things might not be as rigid as we generally think did not surprise them all that much. In fact, if anyone was to be considered to amount to much, they rather expected such things to happen and were apt to be disappointed if they didn't. So what are we to think? Did Jesus actually do at least some of these things that were related about him? Or did his biographers, the "evangelists," simply make them up?

Meier, like may other highly educated believers, appears to be rather cautious, even if not quite to the extent of the skepticism of some biblical "critics" evidenced by the scholars of the much ballyhooed "Jesus Seminar." (We will see more about them later.) Meier's major point in this regard is based on the inescapable fact that most of the sources of whatever we know about Jesus, including the ancient Jewish historian Josephus, attest that Jesus was known as a "healer' and a wonder-worker, so much so that his enemies accused him of being a charlatan or of being in league with the devil.[13] That being said, however, Meier admits that there are three possible ways of explaining all this: either accepting them with unquestioning belief, or explaining them away with rational-scientific explanations, or assigning them mythological-symbolic interpretations. No one tactic can account for *all* of the things the gospels seem to claim to have happened, even if some of them can. Nevertheless, Meier seems willing to admit that some miracle stories may have been made up "whole and entire" to illustrate a particular lesson or point — for example, the rather peculiar story found in both Mark and Matthew about Jesus cursing a barren fig tree and causing it to wither up and die, apparently as a graphic illustration of the coming fate of Jerusalem.[14]

Other stories, such as the seemingly miraculous healings, may have had their origin in events that remain unexplained by science as we know it, much like the apparently unexplained cures at centers of religious pilgrimage in various places around the world.

Finally, Meier admits that some miracles, such as the stories featuring multiplication of loaves and fish, may have begun with an event in which many people were fed from what stores were on hand, but due to the symbolic associations that were made — Jesus as the new Moses feeding his followers in the wilderness — simply got exaggerated in the telling.[15]

No doubt unquestioning believers will find Meier's explanations a bit disappointing. On the other hand, *if* one already believes in a God who presumably created nature, including the rules or laws which govern its workings, who is to question God's decision to temporarily suspend those rules to make a point? After all, if the nature of such a "miracle" (from the Latin *mirare*) is some thing to make us *wonder*, can some point that God wished to make have been made if things were left to business as usual? Even Einstein seems to have weighed in on this subject. When asked about it in 1943, Einstein admitted that although what is written in the Bible about him is "poetically embellished," yet, "It is quite possible that we can do greater things than Jesus."[16]

Thus, in this matter of explaining miracles, signs, and wonders, one wonders in which direction "Occam's razor" — that is, the rule that we should always favor the simplest solution — should cut. Perhaps this is where the discussion of signs, wonders or miracles should lead us — to consider what exactly was the point or what was the lesson that Jesus was trying to make. In other words, what was the overall message that Jesus' mission or ministry was trying to convey?

This question is, beyond any arguments about miracles or their like, the major issue that should most concern us today. Without a careful exploration and even more, with a clear resolution of this question, Christianity, as the movement which claims to be trying to carry on the legacy of Jesus of Nazareth, remains, as it has for some time, in danger of losing its way or becoming irrelevant to the world and its needs; or even worse, guilty of having made the world worse than it need be.

D: The Question of the Kingdom

In the minds of most all scripture scholars and church historians, the real problem posed by the gospels is not so much the miracle stories, but concerns what Jesus meant by the term "the Kingdom of God" or as some translations have it "the Reign of God." In using this kind of language, what was Jesus really talking about?

First of all, to try to answer this question, we have to clear up the confusion caused by the rendition of this idea mostly in the Gospel according to Matthew where the phrase "the Kingdom of Heaven" is used about thirty-three times instead of the term "the Kingdom of God" as found a total of about eighty times in the other synoptic gospels. This is because Matthew's gospel, as was noted earlier, seems to have been intended primarily for a Jewish audience — or more exactly, for congregations made up of Jews who had become Christians. The other gospels, especially those according to Mark and Luke, seem to have been written more for Gentile converts.

It had become, by the time the gospels were written, the custom among Jews to use various substitute words in place of the word for God — particularly the Hebrew word *Yahweh*, the name they believed was revealed, according to the book of Exodus[17], to Moses by God. So it became customary, and still is, for Jews to refer to God as *Adonai* ("Lord") or *Elohim* (a kind of generic word for God or, being in the plural, divine beings in general). Likewise, John's gospel, as well as that of Matthew in the Greek version that has come down to us, often reflects this same reticence by using *ouranou* ("of heaven") instead of *Theou* ("of God").

However, the problem caused by this substitution becomes quickly evident when we recite the Lord's Prayer and really think about what we are actually saying. After all, if we pray "Thy kingdom come, thy will be done, *on earth* as it is in heaven," it seems to make no sense at all unless we are asking that the way things are in heaven become the way things should be here on earth. It should be obvious, then, that the idea that Christianity is all about "saving our souls" or simply working for a reward in the next life is a distortion of the main message. Not that Jesus wasn't promising such a reward, but its fulfillment depends, first, on what we have done here on earth to make this a better place.

If this was, and still is, the case, then the question is *when* and *how* this transformation of earth into God's kingdom or

The Historical Jesus

reign should take place. The controversy is a very old one — even older than the composition of the gospels — if some of Paul's epistles, especially those to the Thessalonians, are any indication of what was very much on the minds of many early converts to Christianity.

Our present version of the Gospel according to Matthew seems to have been based on an earlier but now lost Aramaic collection of the sayings of Jesus that was expanded more or less into a narrative based both on Mark as well as other material also incorporated into Luke's gospel at a later date. However, there continues to be a seemingly endless debate among scholars as to just how many sources, and in what order, entered into the composition of the three "synoptic gospels" of Matthew, Mark, and Luke, although there seems to be unanimous agreement that Mark's is the earliest, despite the tradition, stemming from the 4th century church historian, Eusebius of Caesarea, that Matthew wrote his, in Hebrew (i.e., Aramaic) first.

However, this issue of what Jesus meant by this "Kingdom" became, and still is, an even more hotly debated issue that erupted again with the publication, in 1906, of Albert Schweitzer's book *The Quest of the Historical Jesus*. As its subtitle, *From Reimarus to Wrede*, indicated, it was intended to be a survey of the progress made from the efforts to rediscover Jesus as he really was, beginning with the views of Hermann Reimarus (1714-1769) and extending to those of Georg Wilhelm Wrede (1859-1906). Reimarus, a thoroughgoing deist, had privately discredited Christianity in his own mind, mostly by comparing and analyzing the apparent contradictions in the gospels by uncovering what he suspected were the all-too-human motivations of Jesus and his disciples. Reimarus believed that the disciples, in turn, had concocted a story of Jesus having been resurrected, and eventually recast Christianity as a strictly "spiritual" movement when the second coming of this supposed Messiah failed to materialize.

Reimarus only shared his radical ideas with several close friends, apparently fearing the scandal they would cause. However, the philosopher Gotthold Lessing decided to begin publishing Reimarus' thoughts in a series of articles titled *Fragments by an Anonymous Author* beginning in 1774 — some eight years after Reimarus' death.

The response to Reimarus' views, when they finally became known, seems to have been an attempt to strip the gospels of all their supernatural and miraculous content, and to present a Jesus who worked no miracles and taught bland ethical views that any enlightenment era deist could accept. This same version of Christianity also found expression in Thomas Jefferson's abbreviated version of the gospels where Jesus is presented almost entirely as an ethical philosopher.

However, Wrede, a Lutheran theologian, nearly a century later, returned to take up Reimarus' challenge, but this time armed with much more sophisticated tools of biblical interpretation, concentrating on the Gospel of Mark, with its "messianic secret" and the eschatological, even apocalyptic, expectations of the early Christians addressed in The Second Epistle to the Thessalonians. From his analysis of the latter, Wrede concluded that this second epistle was not written by Paul but by one of Paul's disciples who was among those who were dedicated to adapting the fledgling Christian movement to the non-Jewish world.

Schweitzer, taking up the baton dropped by Wrede's death in 1906, gave us a picture of a prophet of the end-time not unlike John the Baptist who preached the imminent arrival of God's Day of Judgment. But now this fateful day was seen more positively by the early Christians and instead of being

The Historical Jesus

feared, was eagerly awaited as "the Day of the Lord" heralded by Christ's "Second Coming."

This kind of message has been the mainstay of American-style revivalism, even if it pictured a much more human Jesus than that featured in Bible-Belt Christian fundamentalism. In any case, it positively alarmed, if not completely outraged the established churches in Europe. When Schweitzer's book was translated into English in 1910, it was all but banned from the theological schools of the Protestant churches. Meanwhile, the Roman Catholic Church, which had put both of its maverick re-interpreters of Christ and Christianity, Ernest Renan in France and George Tyrrell in England, in their place by excommunication, remained on the sidelines, content to strictly enforce Pius X's crusade against "Modernism." Schweitzer, on the other hand, who was raised and educated as a Lutheran in the Alsace district of Germany (later to become France after World War I), seems to have become disillusioned by the storm his book had created, and gave up any further hopes of a theological teaching career, or even that of a concert-class organist, and went back to school to become a physician, then went on to spend the rest of his life as a medical missionary in Gabon, West Africa. In other words, instead of trying to continue on endless academic controversy over who Jesus really was, Schweitzer decided to imitate how he thought Jesus would act today if faced with a world needing God's mercy and redemption.

Yet the controversy that Schweitzer stirred up still continues, even if the churches still do all they can to conceal it or at least ignore it. This can be especially seen in the treatment given to the gospel passages, mostly found in Mark and in Matthew, about the coming end of the world. Many still take the path begun by Reimarus, even if they attempt to avoid the troubling questions that Reimarus raised. Among these are most of those who make up "the Jesus Seminar," a gathering of about fifty or more scholars who have met periodically to cast their vote on the authenticity of all the various passages in the gospels, first concentrating on the sayings of Jesus and, in their second book, his supposed actions or works. The unusual title of the first volume, *The Five Gospels*, reflects the seminar's decision to include the "Gospel of Thomas," found among the collection of ancient books discovered at Nag Hammadi, Egypt, in 1945. This is because it could conceivably contain some previously unknown but genuine sayings of Jesus — this despite the obviously Gnostic and highly unworldly overtones of some of the passages. For example, the final verse in this supposed gospel has Jesus saying that if he enables Mary Magdalene to become a male, "She too may become a living spirit ... for every female who makes herself male will enter the domain of Heaven."[18]

Given the penchant for philosophic dualism characterizing Gnostic literature, the apocalyptic end-of-the-world type of language found in the three synoptic gospels hardly makes the grade as having been genuine in the eyes of the seminar members. It would definitely make Jesus look like a wild-eyed fanatic instead of the mild-mannered enigmatic wandering sage or homespun Middle-Eastern philosopher. And for all those disturbing passages, well, they are attributed to the evangelists adding some imaginative ideas of their own drawn from the popular apocalyptic passages found in some abundance in late second temple period Judaism. Or else one might actually attribute these words to Jesus, but viewing them as primarily as a prophecy regarding the siege and destruction of Jerusalem. Or perhaps these words about Jerusalem should be taken as a kind of a

The Historical Jesus

preview of what the end of the world might be like when it does finally happen.

Obviously, when one wants to remain an orthodox Christian believer, or even more, trying to help other people to remain such, one is going to be very reluctant to admit that Jesus might have been mistaken about some of these things, or even worse, maybe even a bit deluded. Nevertheless, this possibility will have to be faced when we turn to examining the historical development of Christian beliefs regarding the true identity of Jesus, particularly claims about his divinity, in the next chapter.

In the meantime, the approach taken by N. T. Wright, the acclaimed Anglican expert on the New Testament and early Christian history at Oxford University, could be recommended. Wright seems to be able to admit that Jesus may have been, due to a somewhat foreshortened view of the future, a bit mistaken as to when the "kingdom" that he preached would become a reality and that many early Christians, for this same reason, ended up with somewhat unrealistic views about the Second Coming or as to how it might come about. Yet, Wright insists, that if we are to be truly Christian we must take the ideals put forward by Jesus as serious goals to be achieved, not by waiting for heavenly interventions, but by slow, patient, and untiring perseverance and engagement in the transformation of society into a world that more closely resembles that which Jesus envisioned.

This same sort of idealism and the goals it extols are also, one might add, largely those expressed by the Second Vatican Council in its final major document, the pastoral constitution "On the Church in the Modern World," one of the major achievements of that ground-breaking council before its completion — which in this case should perhaps be seen more as a commencement — in December of 1965.

Einstein, and the Image of God

> Mindful of the Lord's saying: "By this will all men know that you are my disciples, if you have love for one another" (Jn 13:35), Christians cannot yearn for anything more ardently than to serve the men of the modern world with mounting generosity and success. Therefore, by holding faithfully to the Gospel and benefiting from its resources, by joining with every man who loves and practices justice, Christians have shouldered a gigantic task for fulfillment in this world, a task concerning which they must give a reckoning to Him Who will judge every man on the last of days.[19]

Of course, this understanding of the Christian's vocation in the contemporary world is predicated on a vision of faith. So while that vision is based on taking seriously what the historical Jesus may have had to say about his own understanding of what the coming of the Kingdom of God upon this earth might mean for the human race, the possibility of its accomplishment or fulfillment is something else. It depends ultimately on a faith that far transcends the limits of what Jesus accomplished in his short lifetime which ended in an ignominious death on a Roman instrument of torture, the notorious *crux*, reserved for the execution of slaves and subversives.

E. The Death of Jesus and Its Aftermath

Apparently executions by crucifixion were used so often by the procurator or prefect (governor) of the Roman Province of Judea, Pontius Pilate, that he was removed from his position in the year 36. As calculated by evidence provided in part from Flavius Josephus' (37?-95?) *Jewish Antiquities* — even apart from later Christian glosses to Josephus' manuscripts — as well as the *Annuals* complied by the Roman historian Tacitus (56-117?), Meier estimates the death of Jesus as most likely having taken place, in terms of our present calendar, on April 7, 30.[20] While Raymond Brown also admitted this same date as most likely, he did not entirely rule out the possibility of April 3, 33.[21]

Beyond this, we know little for sure about the history surrounding the death of Jesus other than that his followers were soon claiming that he had risen from the dead, and that so vital was his influence, even centuries later, there were those, who, like Mohammed, according to the *Qur'an*, claimed that Jesus had never died.[22]

All this discussion of what Jesus meant by God's "kingdom," as well as Pilate's removal from office after his brutal suppression of a revolt in Samaria raises the old question, lately raised again by Reza Aslan's recent book, as to whether or not Jesus might be considered to have been a "zealot."[23] Aslan seems to have consulted Meier's work regarding this question, making a careful distinction between the broad and narrow sense of the term. Meier points out that there had been a number of various individuals who had opposed the Roman control of Judea from the death of Herod the Great in the year 6. However, according to Meier, the Zealots, the anti-Roman party as described by Josephus as the instigators of the revolt that resulted in the siege and destruction of Jerusalem in the year 70, did not become an organized movement until about the year 68. Moreover, because Judea was only one portion of the Holy Land, Meier has criticized a number of popular books depicting Galilee and the whole of Palestine during the lifetime of Jesus as being under the thumb of Roman occupation, as being, as Meier puts it, "anachronistic," or simply wrong.[24]

On the other hand, if the gospels can be believed as being in any way reliable, there can be no doubt that among the Sadducees, mostly made up of the priestly class in Judea and who were the chief collaborators with the Roman bureaucracy, there were those who plotted or agitated for the death of Jesus. It was these in particular who were all too ready to accuse him as being a subversive and a threat to Roman rule. Of course, some of Jesus' actions in Jerusalem, such as his overturning the money-changers' tables in the temple courtyard — which is placed quite early in John's account of Jesus' public ministry[25] compared to the other gospel accounts — could be seen as being deliberately provocative. But the target of these actions had nothing to do with Roman rule, but with what Jesus considered to be the profanation of God's temple, regarded by all faithful Jews as the holiest spot on earth.

Then we have his triumphal "Palm Sunday" entry into Jerusalem, which seems to have been deliberately intended as a fulfillment of the prophecy found in Zachariah[26] and which is described in the Gospels of both Matthew[27] and of John.[28] Might not this be seen as having been a challenge to the Roman overlords, even though the context of this passage in Zachariah is a message not of rebellion, but of universal peace?

No doubt, as Meier observes[29], there will always be those who are attracted to conspiracy theories, and who like Aslan, will juggle or selectively troll the gospels fishing for evidence to fit their own reconstruction of the story. But in the effort to depict Jesus as a political rebel, how does one discount well-attested and generally accepted as authentic sayings — even by the liberal "Jesus Seminar"[30] — to "Give to the emperor the things that are the emperor's, and to God the things that are God's"?[31] Nevertheless, Aslan tries to interpret this saying as being defiant, even revolutionary, or again, that the puzzling remark about buying swords before he was arrested in the garden of Gethsemane shows that Jesus intended his disciples

The Historical Jesus

to fight off his captors, even though Aslan seems to admit the idea that two swords would hardly have been effective.[32] Or again, how square armed rebellion or even more armed resistance with the injunction not to resist the evildoer, but "If anyone strikes you on the right cheek, turn the other also..." or simply, to "turn the other cheek"?[33]

Certainly, the evangelists in writing their accounts of the life and ministry of Jesus, whom they believed to be the promised Messiah, would have gone out of their way to suppress anything that might have played into the expectations of those who held a very different, even overtly political, view of what the Messiah would be. But even so, if that is the case, then as Meier has observed, regarding the conspiracy theorists, "...we are asked to suppose that the evangelists were surprisingly inept in their cover-up."[34]

Finally, at the end of the third volume of his study of the historical Jesus, Meier speaks of four "enigmas" surrounding him. The first was his relationship to the Mosaic tradition or law; the second, his use of parables; and the third, the mysterious language — especially the phrase or title "the Son of Man" — that Jesus seems to have used regarding himself. In the next chapter we will be looking at that third issue as it bears on the development of Christian beliefs regarding the divinity of Jesus.

Meanwhile, we would best close this chapter on the historical Jesus by admitting, with Meier, that the fourth enigma, "the precise reason(s) why Jesus' life ended as it did, namely by crucifixion at the hands of the Roman prefect on the charge of claiming to be King of the Jews, is the starkest, most disturbing, and the most central of all the enigmas Jesus posed and was."[35]

Of course, as to what happened after that remains, historically speaking, still a matter of debate. On the first level, that of what really happened, we do know for sure that Jesus' followers were soon claiming that he had risen, or more exactly, been "raised" by God's power. We also know that this claim was central to the second level — the *kerygma* or central message of Christianity, for example, as summed up in the liturgical acclamation "Christ has died, Christ is risen, Christ will come again!" However, on the third level, that of the various accounts of Jesus' appearances to the apostles and his disciples as narrated in the gospels, there seems to be, according to *The New Jerome Biblical Commentary*, a wide range of "isolated appearances with little agreement…on circumstances and details."[36] The same commentary also holds to the commonly held opinion today that the last eleven verses of the Gospel according to Mark[37] are a later addition and thus not part of the earliest account which closed with the women disciples fleeing from the empty tomb in "terror and amazement," after being told by a "young man…dressed in a white robe" that "He has been raised" and that they will "see him in Galilee … "just as he told you."[38]

The same commentary also holds the opinion that Chapter 21 of John's Gospel, which details Jesus' appearances to Peter and the rest of the apostles in Galilee, is by a different author than the accounts of his appearances to them in Jerusalem as narrated in Chapter 20. So it seems clear that here we are dealing more with a subject to be discussed in the next chapter, "The Christ of Christian Tradition" or in other words "The Christ of Faith."

Conclusion

If the third of the four "enigmas" with which Meier closed his third volume of his massive study has to do with what Jesus meant by his self-assumed title "the Son of Man," and the

The Historical Jesus

fourth enigma is as why he met the fate he did, need the mystery be seen to be all that great? Here we should credit Aslan with stressing the connection between these two enigmas, even if Aslan is probably wrong about what Jesus understood about what we might call "messiahship" and about what he called "the Kingdom of God."[39] Whether or not Aslan actually read Reimarus is not clear, but if he had, he should have paid more attention to a very interesting observation regarding what Jesus may have seen as his fate.

In Chapter IV about what Reimarus called the "pretense" or mistaken view in the early church that Jesus would soon return, Reimarus wrote:

> First, it should be known that the Jews themselves had two different systems of their Messiah. Most of them, indeed, expected in such a person a worldly sovereign, who should release them from slavery, and make other nations submit to them. In this system there was nothing but splendor and glory, no previous suffering, no return; the long-wished for kingdom was to begin immediately upon the coming of the Messiah. However, there were some few others who said their Messiah would come twice, and each time in a quite different manner. The first time he would appear in misery, and would suffer and die. The second time he would come in the clouds of Heaven and receive unlimited power.[40]

As transcribed by Lessing, Reimarus seems to have added that this idea of a "double Messiah," or even two different messiahs, is mentioned in the writing of the second century Christian apologist Justin Martyr in his *Dialogue with Trypho*[41] and was even further elaborated by Jews even in Reimarus' own time. Some scholars believe that the same idea has since then also been discovered in the Dead Sea Scrolls.[42]

Einstein, and the Image of God

If this was the case, then should we be surprised if Jesus, convinced that he had been chosen by God to be the Messiah — even though he avoided saying so lest he be misunderstood as a political revolutionary — seems to have also been convinced, at least within a year or so after the beginning of his public ministry, that he would suffer a violent death? And when he did, who can blame his followers, or even Jesus himself, from expecting that he would return, even during the lifetime of some of those who had heard his prediction?

However, if one wants to remain a traditional Christian believer, one is apt to be very reluctant to admit that Jesus may have been mistaken about some of these things. Nevertheless, this possibility will have to be faced when we turn to examining the historical development of Christian beliefs regarding the true identity of Jesus, particularly Christian claims that he was, and still is, divine.

---

[1] Matt 11:27; Luke 10:22; see also John 3:11.
[2] Jammer, Max. *Einstein and Religion*, 19.
[3] Calaprice, Alice, *The Ultimate Quotable Einstein*, 325.
[4] Jammer, 22.

The Historical Jesus

[5] Fitzmyer, John A. *Scripture and Christology*, 1986.
[6] Rom 1:3.
[7] Gal 4:4.
[8] Quoted in Matt 2:6.
[9] Matt 2:15b.
[10] John 1:1-14.
[11] Formerly known as "The Holy Office of the Inquisition."
[12] Meier, Joseph P. *A Marginal Jew*, Part Three of Volume II, Chapters 17 and 18.
[13] Meier II, 967.
[14] Mark 11:12-14; Matt 21: 18-19.
[15] Meier, III, 968
[16] Calaprice, Alice. *The Ultimate Quotable Einstein*, 337.
[17] Exod 3:14.
[18] Thom 114.
[19] *The Teachings of the Second Vatican Council*, Newman Press, 1966, 555-56.
[20] Meier, I, 402.
[21] Brown, Raymond, *The Death of the Messiah*, II, 1376).
[22] Surah 4:157-58.
[23] Aslan, Reza. *Zealot: The Life and Tomes of Jesus of Nazareth*, 2013.
[24] Meier, III, 632-33.
[25] John 2:13-25.
[26] Zach 9: 9-10.
[27] Matt 21:5
[28] John 12:15.
[29] Ibid., 567.
[30] Funk et al. *The Five Gospels*, 102, 236, 378, 526.
[31] Mark 12:17; Matt 22:21; Luke 20:25; Thom 100:2.
[32] Aslan, 76-78.
[33] Matt 5:39; Luke 6:29.
[34] Meier, III, 566.
[35] Meier, III, 646.
[36] Brown, Fitzmyer, & Murphy, 81: 127.
[37] Mark 16:9-20.
[38] Mark 16:5-8.
[39] Aslan, 136-45.

[40] Lessing, *Fragments*, LXXXVI.
[41] *Dialogue with Trypho,* Chapters XXXII and XXXIII.
[42] For a Jewish perspective on this see comments by Rabbi Moshe Reiss: www.moshereiss.org/christianity/04_deadsea/04_deadsea.html (accessed 1/14/2015).

Chapter 5
The Christ of Christian Tradition

As a preliminary note to this chapter, it should be said that the same distinctions made by the Vatican's Biblical commission regarding the three levels of tradition found in the gospels could be extended to the whole of the New Testament, indeed, probably to the whole Bible. But for now, suppose we just look at the epistles or letters of the New Testament from this same perspective, distinguishing as far as possible, the first level (what really happened) from the second level (the *kerygma* or basic message), from the third level (the development of thought or interpretation used by the particular author or school of thought).

Looked at from that perspective, it is obvious that, aside from the repetition of the basic message, most of the material in the New Testament epistles, particularly those attributed to Paul and his followers, falls into the third category, which is the elaboration of the basic message, usually in terms that the writer thought most suited to the particular historical and social circumstances, or the immediate needs of the audience in mind.

Next, it should also be noted that the authentic letters written by Paul — these being the epistles to the Galatians, 1 & 2 Corinthians, Romans and 1 Thessalonians — are generally considered to be older than any of the four "canonical" or accepted gospels that we have today, while 2 Thessalonians remains disputed.[1] Those other epistles written by his disciples or others inspired by his themes — for example Colossians, and Ephesians, and the "pastoral epistles" to Timothy and Titus — are generally referred to as being "Pauline." This realization is very important for an accurate understanding of the development of the Christian teachings regarding the mission of Jesus in his role as the Messiah or "Christ." That being said, we can now proceed, first by summarizing the situation as it stands today.

A: The Historical Question Revisited

The possibility, indeed, the likelihood that Jesus was greatly mistaken in his belief that he, "the Son of Man," would soon be seen returning on "the clouds of heaven"[2] to usher in the final age, or the end of the world was, for Reimarus, and still remains, if Aslan is in any way typical of the mood today, the final road-block against any acceptance of the central Christian belief — that Jesus was, or for that matter still is, the Son of God, the incarnation of God Almighty.

While the resurrection of Jesus from his grave can be disputed, it cannot be disproved: it is, in a sense, as the Russian philosopher and theologian, Nicolai Berdyaev, said, "meta-historical." But a "Second Coming" especially one that seems to have been promised by Jesus within the life-span of at least some of his hearers[3] is quite another matter. As a result, many commentators on the gospels are inclined to see the prediction of the return of the Christ as associated with those gospel passages as having been confused with a prophecy of the destruction of Jerusalem by the Romans in the year 70, or only to have been written after the fact. In any case, we know that at the time of that national disaster no one saw or even claimed to see Jesus returning on the clouds of heaven. As a result, even traditional believers have postponed the Second Coming of Christ to the end of the world, or have continued to be wrong when they were rash enough to predict it was about to happen.

On the other hand, it still remains, as we have seen in the previous chapter, a matter of debate over just exactly what this title of "Messiah" or "Christ", actually meant in terms of Jesus' announcement or proclamation of the arrival of "the Kingdom of God" or "the Kingdom of Heaven."

On one side of the debate are those, as was Schweitzer and Wrede, and before them, Reimarus, who are convinced that Jesus expected the coming of the kingdom to occur shortly, even within the lifetime of his first disciples. On the other side are those who either believe that the rather apocalyptic language attributed to Jesus, especially in the Gospels of Matthew and Mark, is not what in fact Jesus said, or else are forced to concede that if he said these things, at least as a human being, Jesus was mistaken, except perhaps regarding the destruction of Jerusalem. In either case, the upshot was that, as the saying — sometimes attributed to Schweitzer himself — goes: "Jesus preached the Kingdom of God and [when it didn't come] the Apostles preached Christ."

B: From Paul to John

Generally speaking, most modern scripture scholars have held to the theory that, to begin with, belief in Jesus as the Messiah or the Christ only gradually grew into the conviction that Jesus, having been raised from the dead, became, at least for us, equal to being God in a human form. Accordingly, whether one begins with the Gospel according to Mark as being the earliest gospel, or with the authentic letters of Paul as being the earliest New Testament documents, and ends with the Gospel according to John or the pseudo-Pauline letters such a Colossians, Ephesians, or even Hebrews, one is supposed to see a gradual development of belief in the divinity of Christ. Or to put the same idea in the language nowadays often used by Christian theologians, the original "Low Christology" or "Christology of Ascent"—where Jesus begins as human just like us, but eventually reaches the state of becoming divine — is gradually replaced, in the later books of the New Testament, by a "High Christology" or "Christology of Descent" where the divine and eternal "Word of God" eventually becomes "incarnate" — that is to say, he is seen to have descended or lowered himself to take upon himself human form.

This view of a gradual development seems logical enough, given the human tendency to elaborate or even exaggerate, especially regarding those things or those persons we see to be of major importance to our lives. The problem is that this neat and logical scenario does not quite fit the facts.

On the one hand, in the epistles of Paul that have always been considered authentic, the apostle never goes so far as to identify Jesus or Christ as being God outright and that instead, for Paul, Jesus is "the Son of God." Accordingly, Paul appears to have generally taken the precaution of referring to God — that is, as we might say, "Almighty God" — as *ho Theos*, literally "*the* God," with the article pointedly referring to the one and only God that Jesus called "Father."

Nevertheless, this distinction between "the God" and "the Son of God" is not as hard and fast as it may seem, because for Paul, Jesus is also the *Kyrios* or "Lord." This was the title used in the Greek version of the Old Testament to translate *Adonai*, which was one of the Hebrew words used (as explained in the previous chapter) as a substitute in place of God's most sacred personal name, *Yahweh*.

Furthermore, as the contemporary American scholar of the New Testament, Bart Ehrman — who currently classifies himself as an agnostic — has recently pointed out, we have the so-called "hymn" or poem found in the second chapter of Paul's Epistle to the Philippians, which begins with the words "Although he [Jesus] was in form equal to God" and then goes on to describe how Jesus "emptied himself, taking on the form of a servant ... even undergoing death, death on a cross."

Certainly this sounds like a "High Christology" similar to that found in the Gospel of John, or in the "hymns" or poems of praise incorporated into other epistles, particularly those to the Colossians and Ephesians, that are considered to be Pauline in inspiration but most likely written some years after Paul's death by someone else. As a result, during one period in the recent past, the Epistle to the Philippians was also considered by some to be "pseudo-Pauline" in that sense. However, both Ehrman and other contemporary experts no longer hold that to be the case, and instead believe that Paul himself incorporated this short poem or "hymn," which they believe predates Paul.[4] Ehrman and others also point out that the second part or stanza of this hymn or poem contrasts this "emptying out" or *kenosis* of Christ in contrast to his later exaltation or glorification — a theme which seems to balance the *descent* associated with the seeming "High Christology" of the beginning of the passage with a note of final *ascent*.

The only other possible exception to these general observations concerning the status of Christ in respect to God in the Pauline writings is in the Epistle to Titus, 2:13. In that instance, the NRSV translation ends that passage with the phrase "of our great God and Savior, Jesus Christ" but, in a footnote, gives as an alternate ending "of the great God and our Savior, [Jesus Christ]" and seems to favor this alternative reading as being the most likely. But again, it should be noted that many authorities, for other reasons, do not ascribe this Epistle to Titus, as well as those addressed to Timothy, as having been personally written by St. Paul, but again by a disciple some years later, after Paul's death, in the year 64.

However, Ehrman, in his analysis of how Jesus gradually "became God"[5] in the eyes of Christians, features an interesting sidelight which may help us understand the gradual shift from the apparently "Low Christology" of the earliest documents to the "High Christology" that we find in the later writings attributed to the Apostle John. It is the view that Jesus was an "angel" sent by God. Ehrman points to the phrase found in Paul's Epistle to the Galatians, where Paul commends the Galatians for having received him (Paul) "as an angel" sent by God, just as they had received Christ.[6]

As improbable as Ehrman's interpretation of this passage may seem, we know that among some early Christians, this kind of identification of Jesus — known today as an "Angel Christology" — was apparently the case. In fact it may have been the reason that the First Epistle of John comes out so strongly in condemning those who refused to believe that Jesus actually came to us "in the flesh" and brands those who deny this to be "not from God."[7] We also know that this kind of interpretation of Christ was said to have been held by the "Ebionite" Christians, Christians of Jewish descent who had fled across the Jordan to escape from Jerusalem before its destruction. This opinion in turn seems to have gradually morphed into what was known later as the Docetist heresy, which held that Jesus really wasn't a human being, but only appeared (*dokein,* or "to seem") to be human.

The problem with Ehrman's interpretation, however, is whether or not Paul was taking the word "angel" (*aggelos*) in its literal sense of "messenger" or instead a separate spirit-beings in its own right, which seems to have been a belief acquired by Judaism during its exile in Babylon. This would also follow from the view taken by theologian Jack Mahoney, SJ, in his book *Christianity in Evolution,* which could be seen as backed up by Robert North, SJ, where North explained how the Hebrew *mal'āk,* originally meaning an "ambassador," "envoy," or "messenger," eventually became thought of as a

The Christ of Christian Tradition

heavenly being, probably due to Persian influence toward the end of the period of the exile.[8]

This term *mal'āk* was eventually translated into Greek as *aggelos* — from the verb *aggelō* meaning "to announce." So it is easy to see how Paul might have described Christ as an "angel" in the first and more original sense of that word. But it is hard to imagine Paul as applying that later meaning to Christ, even if Paul, like most of the Pharisees, contrary to the Saducees, believed that angels existed as a distinct class of celestial beings.[9]

In any case, it would seem that if an "Angel Christology" had begun to become popular in certain segments of the early Christian world, this might also explain why what theologians call the "High Christology" found so strongly in the Johannine writings is paradoxically a Christology that emphasizes the *descent* of God's "Word" or expression of himself in this world. This Christology would emphasize his not just being human in form (*morphe*) or outward appearance but in actuality, "in the flesh," that is, in the blood and guts reality of human existence. Thus it is that we find what is perhaps the most arresting confession of faith in the divinity of Jesus expressed not just in the prologue of John's Gospel, but in the next-to-last chapter when the risen Christ bids his doubting apostle, Thomas, to probe the wounds in his hands and side.[10] It is this which elicits perhaps the most outspoken confession of faith in that whole gospel, Thomas' outburst: "My Lord and my God!" It is for this reason that the Gospel according to John, the last to be written, is generally considered to be the least bashful about asserting Christ's divinity — earning its author the description "the theologian" in the Eastern Orthodox tradition.

However, these contrasting approaches to understanding Jesus did not end with the Apostolic era, which tradition holds to have closed with the death of John the Apostle around the end of the first century. Shortly after that, we will see the beginnings of two "schools" or centers of early Christian thought, one located in or centered around the now defunct city of Antioch in Syria, the other associated with the still-thriving port city of Alexandria in Egypt.

C: From Antioch to Alexandria

After the destruction of Jerusalem by the Romans, Antioch, where the followers of Jesus had been first called "Christians" and from where Paul and Barnabas had set out on the first sea-journey mission to foreign lands[11], soon became the center of Christian missionary activity. According to early church traditions, even Peter had spent some time there before joining Paul in Rome where they were both eventually martyred during the persecution unleashed by Nero.[12]

The next significant voice associated with Antioch was that of its Christian leader or "bishop," Ignatius, who tradition holds that, along with Polycarp — who eventually became bishop of the church in Smyrna — were both disciples of the apostle John. Although there are many letters that have been attributed to Ignatius, some of which are considered spurious, there are seven of these letters that are considered by most authorities to be authentic, all of them written while Ignatius was being taken to Rome to be executed by the order of Emperor Trajan in the year 110. In his "Letter to the Romans"[13], Ignatius expresses his wish, lest any influential Christians in Rome attempt to save him, that they "suffer me to copy the passion of my God."[14] Clearly this is a reference to the divinity of Jesus, yet qualified — by the possessive pronoun "my" — again reflecting Paul's and even John's hesitation, despite the many hints of his divine qualities to identify Christ as being identical to God almighty, or to use Paul's expression, "the God" (*ho Theos*).

However, even given this distinction between "my God" and "the God," this still leaves us with the challenge of the famous "I am" sayings found in John's gospel, among them "I am the way, the truth, and the life"[15], "I am the bread of life"[16], "I am the light of the world"[17], and that which most clearly points to his divinity; "Before Abraham came to be, I am."[18] It is the boldness of these sayings, with their veiled allusion to the most sacred name of God — *Yahweh*[19] — and which are uncharacteristic of the other three gospels, that drives most New Testament scholars to the conclusion that the bulk of John's Gospel belongs to the third level tradition as outlined by the Vatican's Biblical Commission.

Yet, at this point in the history of early Christianity there still seems to be no real division over the identity of Jesus Christ. Ignatius's view of Christ, even if he was personally instructed by John, seems to have been no different than Paul's. Jesus was seen to be both truly human and truly divine. The problem was over the path through which he came to be recognized as such. By the middle of the second century, however, there are signs that the approach being taken in the church in Alexandria, which was supposedly founded by St. Mark, reputed to have acted as a secretary to St. Peter and the author of the first gospel, was somewhat different than that being used in Antioch.

This difference might be seen as due to the intellectual atmosphere of Alexandria, considered to be, in respect to its rival, Athens, the other capitol of learning in the ancient world. It had what was reputed to be the greatest library in the world — at least until a succession of fires — the first caused by Julius Caesar's attempt to put down a revolt, and the last, in 391, caused by Coptic Christians intent on destroying pagan temples — eventually reduced its collections to ashes.

Alexandria also was the city where Jewish scholars had first translated the Hebrew Scriptures into Greek, and where the Jewish philosopher, Philo, had begun, around the time that Jesus lived in Galilee, to explain Jewish beliefs in terms that those educated in Greek philosophy might better understand.

Accordingly, there should be little wonder over the fact that the Christian school of learning that began to become evident in Alexandria around the middle of the third century would show a great preference for has been described as the "High Christology" found in the Johannine writings in the New Testament. In this the Alexandrian Christians were quite naturally following in the footsteps of Philo, who had even used the Greek concept of the divine *Logos* ("Reason" or "Word") to explain, or even translate the Hebrew word *hochma* which had already been translated as *Sophia* ("Wisdom") in the Greek version of the Old Testament. Likewise, we find Clement, Bishop of Alexandria (c.150-215), appealing to Stoic ethical reasoning, with its concept of natural law or ethics, to interpret the biblical commandments, and the priest Origen of Alexandria (c.185-254), in turn, employing Platonist concepts to interpret Holy Scripture in general. However, eventually Origen seems to have moved a bit too far into his Platonism with his ideas of the preexistence of souls, reincarnation and universal restoration, and ended up fleeing to Palestine for refuge.

Origen's problems at home should have been a warning to another Alexandrian priest, Arius, who was born just a few years (c. 250) before Origen is said to have died. Arius had become noted for his talent of composing hymns and other forms of popular literature that were designed to present theological, or more exactly Christological, ideas in forms derived from Platonism. We don't have much of anything he wrote except by way of his being quoted (or misquoted?) by his enemies, but what we do have seems to suggest that Arius wanted to call Jesus "divine" but in a kind of secondary sense by appealing to Platonic notions of a high-God ("The One") contrasted to quasi-god or "demiurge" through whom the universe was created. According to his critics, Arius had also quoted the passage in the Gospel according to John, where Jesus says "the Father is greater than I,"[20] to argue that Christ's divinity was of lesser rank, and to the Epistle to the Colossians where Christ is described as "the firstborn of creation"[21] to assert that he was a creature like ourselves. Furthermore, Arius asserted that Christ possessed a different nature or *ousia* (literally "stuff" but more often translated as "substance") than God.

The ideas being spread by Arius proved to be very popular, and were even being adopted by quite a number of bishops, despite the fact that in 320 the Bishop of Alexandria, called a council of over a hundred Egyptian and Libyan bishops, who excommunicated Arius, who in turn fled from Egypt to take refuge with his friend Bishop Eusebius of Nicomedia in Asia Minor.

Meanwhile, the Christian intellectual atmosphere in and around Antioch seems to have, in contrast to that of Alexandria, begun to place more and more emphasis on the human aspects of Jesus, especially on a "Low Christology," even to the point of being expressed in what has been called "adoptionist" terms or, in milder words nowadays, as "Spirit Christology." This approach, in its full-blown form, held that until the descent of the Holy Spirit upon Jesus at his baptism in the river Jordan, as described in the gospels[22], he was merely a human being like the rest of us. Or in another variation of this same approach, this special adoption of the human Jesus to become truly God's son, took place at the moment of his conception in the womb of Mary as described in Luke's gospel.[23] In fact, this view seems to have been similar to that held by Lactantius (c. 240-330), who was a theological advisor to Emperor Constantine. For Lactantius, the divine qualities of Christ were explained by the indwelling of God's Holy Spirit — not seen so much as a "person," but as a power — in the man Jesus.

D: Constantine's Intervention

In 306, Constantine had followed his father as ruler of the western half of the Roman Empire in 312, after winning a battle at the Milvian Bridge outside Rome. Although not a Christian himself, he credited his victory to the power of Christ, and succeeded in taking over the eastern half of the empire as well, officially granting Christianity the right to exist the following year with the Edict of Toleration — also known as "The Edict of Milan." Soon after, Constantine decided, in order to better govern his wide-reaching empire, to move the administrative center of the empire eastward to a Greek colony called *Byzantium* on the Straits of Bosporus where Europe and Asia Minor meet — which city was eventually renamed Constantinople. It was from this vantage point that he began to be alarmed by all this theological quarrelling and its potential to fracture his newly reunited empire.

Accordingly, with the advice of another friend and advisor, Bishop Hosios of Cordova, Constantine decided to call a general, world-wide or "ecumenical" council at the nearby town of Nicea to be held during the beginning of the summer of 325. Of the some 1800 bishops invited, however, only about 300, or at most possibly 318, actually attended, most of them, all but five, from the eastern part of the empire. Two priests from Rome also attended to represent Pope Sylvester I. Constantine himself is said to have sat in the middle of the assembly in shining robes and jeweled splendor, not taking part in the deliberations, but with his imperial guard discretely standing in the wings to make sure things remained orderly. Bishop Hosios chaired the assembly.

The result of the deliberations at Nicea was that although about twenty-two bishops favored Arius' point of view, nevertheless in the end all but two signed the statement of faith, which was essentially modeled on the traditional baptismal creeds (similar to the "Apostles' Creed") but which, regarding the divinity of Jesus, included the additional phrases: "God from true God, Light from True Light, consubstantial with the Father."

Nevertheless, the term "consubstantial" or (in Greek) *homoousios*, had especially proved contentious, partly because Arius had been the first to use the word *ousia* to describe the nature of Jesus, which he insisted was different than that of God. However, Arius' friend Eusebius of Nicomedia, and another Eusebius, the church historian who was Bishop of Caesarea in Palestine, were able to convince the majority that in using the compound adjective *homoousios*, they could affirm that Christ shared the same divine nature as the Father, but at the same time be personally distinct from Him.[24] But there were still others who would have preferred to add the proverbial "one *iota*" to the term to have it come out as *homoiousios*, meaning "similar to" but not exactly the same. This particular matter of the exact wording of the Nicene Creed and the controversy surrounding it deserves our special attention because it was to remain a key factor in the disputes which continued to rock the Church and disrupt its unity for generations, even centuries, afterward.

Einstein and the Image of God

"Arianism," as it has been called, continued to flourish in many areas of the Christian world, not only those out of the direct control of the Roman Empire, but even for periods of time within it. For example, Constantius, Constantine's son and heir to the imperial throne, was outspokenly an "Arian" in his views. And many bishops still had some sympathy for what Arius had attempted to do, even if they didn't agree with the language or philosophical means with which he attempted it. And as for those who sided with the two bishops who had tried to defend Arius, these were accused of being either "Eusebians" or "semi-Arians." One of the latter was St. Cyril, Patriarch of Jerusalem, who although he was not a bishop back in 325, nevertheless was present to sign the ratification and further expansion of the Nicene Creed at the First Council of Constantinople in 381.

Yet this was hardly the end of the dispute. The lure of using Plato's ideas to try to comprehend Christian beliefs was still strong. Because Plato had taught that there were several parts to the human soul, another theologian, Apollinaris of Laodicea (died c. 390), suggested another approach to what Arius had been trying to accomplish — that is, to safeguard the distinction between God and Jesus, yet safeguard his unity with God — could be better accomplished by assuming that the highest part of Christ's human soul — what the Platonists called the "rational soul" — had been replaced by the divine Word, but that everything else about him was strictly human. But as the critics of Apollinaris pointed out, this would imply that Jesus had no rational or complete human nature. And so the seeds of dissention sowed by Arius continued and still do continue in one form or another even now.

Because of the seeming victory of the Alexandrine theology at Nicea over its home-grown heretic Arius, it is not surprising that those bishops who leaned more in the direction of the Antiochian school were still to be heard from. One of these, Nestorius, an abbot from Antioch who had become the archbishop or Patriarch of Constantinople, was said to have even gone so far to claim that it improper or theologically inaccurate to speak of Mary as being "The Mother of God" when, indeed, she had only been, strictly speaking, the mother of Jesus. In other words, Nestorius seemed to be making a clear distinction between Jesus as a human being on the one hand, and his identity or role as the Christ, the Son of God, on the other. This opinion was seen, especially by St. Cyril of Alexandria, as being subversive of the Nicene understanding, and Nestorius, in turn, accused Cyril of being an Apollinarian — a charge which, not surprisingly, Cyril denied.

As a result of that latest theological quarrel, and largely due to Cyril's efforts, still another general council was called, this time at Ephesus in 431, again under imperial oversight. Thus, what has been named the Third Ecumenical Council, or The Council of Ephesus, solemnly defined Mary as *Theotokos*, a title which, literally translated, means "God-bearer" or [she] "who gives birth to God," but which was, again on the popular or more devotional level, rendered as "Mother of God" — this without any fine distinctions between simply giving birth and all the rest that is fully implied by the knowledge we now have of biological motherhood. But the Christian Churches to the east were, perhaps partly for political reasons — being geographically outside the empire — notable for their non-compliance with the Council of Ephesus, and as a result, were long-time labeled as being "Nestorian."

Einstein and the Image of God

E: The Chalcedonian Compromise

However, this division between what was then known as Catholic Christianity on the one hand, and, on the other hand, the Christian church in countries east of the empire was not to be the last. Where those who were sympathetic to Nestorius tended to stress two separate natures, the human and the divine, within Christ, those who reacted most strongly against this view, who were most closely tied to the traditions of the church in Alexandria, started to speak of a single, as it were, fused or amalgamated divine-human nature. For this reason they were soon called *monophysites*, thus leading to further tension and even lesser hopes of healing the schism between those who considered themselves to be "orthodox" and those who sided with the Nestorians. As a result, again another council was convened, this time in 451 at Chalcedon, again, just across the Bosporus from Constantinople. There it was solemnly declared, closely following the suggestions spelled out in a letter from the Bishop of Rome, Pope Leo ("Leo the Great"), that Christ should be seen as consisting of two distinct natures united in one single person who is both "consubstantial with the Father in his divinity and consubstantial with us in his humanity."[25]

However, instead of the desired healing of the schism involving the Nestorians, the result of the Chalcedon formula was yet another schism. The monophysite party seems to have been particularly put off by the further explanation given by the Chalcedon formula, namely: "The distinction between natures was never abolished by their union, but rather the character proper to each was preserved as they came together in one person (*prosōpon*) and one hypostasis."

We have already seen some of the problems that have arisen around the use of the first term (*prosōpon*) when it began to be used in regard to God as a trinity. But this time it was the second term, *hypostasis* that seems to have caused the trouble. So, this time it was the Egyptian "Coptic" Church and its sister Church in Abyssinia (Ethiopia and Eritrea) which were most noticeable for their refusal to comply with the Chalcedonian formula, apparently because according to their understanding of these words, it sounded to them like Chalcedon was weakening the union between the divine and human aspects of Christ, rather than strengthening it. So to the monophysites, the Greek and Latin churches appeared to be "diaphysites" and they did not hesitate to say so. Eventually a number of Christian churches in the East, including those in Armenia, Iraq, Persia and India and calling themselves "Oriental Orthodox," sided with the Alexandrine church, hence all appearing to be "monophysite" in the eyes of the Greeks and Latins. But there can be little doubt that much of it was driven by both civil as well as ecclesiastical politics.

Nor was this fractiousness — with each party branding its opposites as "heretics"— the end of the story. Further divisions arose, even among the adherents to the Chalcedonian belief, over whether or not Christ had one will or two, thus practically speaking, leading to further debates over whether or not he could have been truly tempted or even, at least humanly speaking, ignorant of some things, like, for example, just when the world would come to an end. So yet another council, this time the Sixth Ecumenical Council — the Third Council of Constantinople — was called in 681, this time to suppress the heresy called *monothelitism* (literal translation: "one-will-ism").

Conclusion

This last matter as simply one more instance of where the Chalcedonian formula or definition has become, for all

Einstein and the Image of God

practical purposes, the Chalcedonian or "Christological Problem" *par excellence*. For all its precision, all that the Council of Chalcedon seems to have achieved was define Christian belief about the nature and the person of Christ in a way that makes the whole matter all the more mysterious, and in terms retaining a balanced understanding, all the more impossible. It is rather like standing in the exact center of a teeter-totter or see-saw and trying to keep it level: the very least movement of ones head or even ones finger is apt to throw it off balance. From time to time, a theoretical balance may have been achieved, but practically speaking, history shows that retaining that balance has been all but impossible.

One further instance of this might be seen in the outbreak of "Iconoclasm" in the seventh century, mainly in the eastern regions of Asia Minor bordering and including Armenia. From about the second century on, the use of icons (from the Greek *eikōn*) of Christ, and of Mary and the other saints, had grown increasingly popular, almost to the point where abuses — like the substitution of icons in place of godparents at baptism — had begun to occur. And by the seventh century, other factors had also begun to play a role. During the century that followed Mohammed's flight to Medina in 622, Islam, with its total rejection of images, had all but conquered most of the Middle East and North Africa. One is left with the impression that by then Christianity, especially in the Middle East, had become nearly totally exhausted by internal disputes that had, by then only confused many Christian believers and made them an easy target for a much simpler faith.

Meanwhile, to add to the confusion, a rather strange amalgam of Christianity and Gnostic dualism known as "Paulicianism" had broken out, again in the eastern part of Asia Minor. It was a doctrine that was almost Manichaean in its rejection of anything material or fleshly as the creation of the devil and that spiritual people should have nothing to do with it, including rituals and sacraments like Baptism or the Eucharist. All this would seem to have had implications, even if not consciously drawn out, about any belief in a God who had taken a human identity, or even more, had suffered and died for our sake. Thus, the Second Council of Nicea (the Seventh Ecumenical Council) was convened in 787, to defend the use of sacred images. For, as the assembled bishops decreed, this use of images "... confirms that the incarnation of the Word of God was real and not imaginary and to our benefit as well, for realities that illustrate each other undoubtedly reflect each other's meaning."[26] In other words, the image of God made man serves also as a reflection of humanity made "in the image and likeness of God."[27]

Yet it could be instructive to note that the only forms of Christianity that seem to have survived for long in some parts of the Islamic world cut off for centuries, especially from both the Western (Catholic) and Byzantine (Orthodox) churches, were those churches that had adopted one or the other easier to understand views that the Catholic and Orthodox churches both considered to be heretical. Thus most of those to the east of what had been the Byzantine Empire were considered to be Nestorian (adoptionist) in belief, while to the south, the Coptic or Egyptian Church, as well as its sister church in Ethiopia, remained resolutely monophysite (although they prefer the term "miaphysite"[28]), never having subscribed to the Council of Chalcedon. And even recent discussions that have taken place between Catholic, Orthodox and Coptic theologians have been said to have reached the point where any differences that remain are not substantially real but mostly semantic.

If that is the case, what else might we conclude? Might it not be safe to say that today most Christian believers —

Einstein and the Image of God

whether they are Catholic, Orthodox, or traditional Protestants — are all, practically speaking, more or less monophysites without realizing it, as if God had only pretended to take on human form? And if that is the case, would it not confirm Einstein's view that the majority of people need to think of God in personal terms, even if that "person" is not seen as really being human like us? Or is it that if this person appears to be too human, subject to all our human weaknesses, whether physical, psychological, or even spiritual — think of Jesus' cry of despair on the cross — we would lose faith in his power to save?

This, I think, is the dilemma still faced by Christianity, to still convince the world that Jesus really did make or really can make a difference — because, as St. Paul put it to the Corinthians "in Christ God was reconciling the world to himself." [29] Or as many of the Church's earliest theologians saw it, "What was not assumed [by Christ] was not redeemed." In other words, the essence of Christianity lies in the fullest possible reality of the Incarnation of God in our humanity.

---

[1] Brown, Fitzmyer and Murphy, *New Jerome Biblical Commentary*, 48:6-7
[2] Matt 26:64.
[3] Matt 24:3; Mark 13:30; Luke 21:32-33.
[4] Brown, Fitzmyer & Murphy, 68: 3-10.
[5] Ehrman, Bart D. *How Jesus Became God: The Exaltation of a Jewish Preacher from Galilee.*
[6] Gal 2:52.
[7] 1 John 4:3-4.
[8] Brown, Fitzmyer & Murphy, 23:34.
[9] Acts 24:10-27.

[10] John 20:28.
[11] Acts 11:26; 13:14.
[12] Quasten, Johannes, *Patrology*, Vol. I, 49-50).
[13] Ignatius, Rom 6:3.
[14] Kleist, James A. *The Epistles of St. Clement of Rome and St. Ignatius of Antioch*, 135, n. 21.
[15] John 14:6.
[16] John 6:35.
[17] John 8:12.
[18] John 8:58.
[19] Exod 3:14. It is believed that, etymologically speaking, this sacred name is derived from the Hebrew phrase *Ehyeh asher ehyeh* ("I am who/what I am") which in the third person, is pronounced as *Jaweh*.
[20] John 14:28.
[21] Col 1:15b.
[22] Matt 3:13-17; Mark 1:1-11; Luke 3:21-22.
[23] Luke 1:26-28.
[24] Grillmeier, Aloys. *Christ in the Christian Tradition*, Vol. I, 149.
[25] *Catechism of the Catholic Church*, #467: quote from Denzinger 302.
[26] *Catechism of the Catholic Church.*, #1160; Council of Nicea II: Denzinger 600.
[27] Gen 1:26.
[28] Meaning two identities, the divine and human, merged into a single nature, but without separation, confusion, or alteration.
[29] 2 Cor 5:19.

Einstein and the Image of God

Chapter 6
The Christ of the Future

If theology is faith seeking understanding, then we must be aware that that the tools of that understanding, and the understandings that they produce, are apt to be shaped by the prevailing habits of thought of any particular place and era. We have already seen, in the previous chapter, how the early Christian school of thought centered in Antioch tended to think and express itself in terms of the down-to-earth biblical style of stories and examples found in the first three gospels. In contrast to Antioch, the theologians in Alexandria, steeped in the atmosphere of Greek learning, were drawn to a more abstract approach, particularly one that drew on the Platonist roots and Stoic expressions of what was then the prevailing philosophy.

However, we must remember that whether those tools and habits of thought were biblically-based, or on the other hand more philosophically shaped, both depended on a particular world-view or cosmology. The basic biblical world-view was, to be blunt about it, pre-scientific. It still, as in the book of Genesis, pictured the earth as being flat, with the heavens thought of as something like an inverted bowl overhead, and with it all shaped by God in the relatively recent past.

In contrast, the philosophical cosmology of the first few centuries of our era was relatively scientific, in that it was rooted in careful observations and mathematical calculations, such as those made by the Alexandrine scholar Ptolemy (c. 90-168) thus almost a contemporary of St. Clement and Origen. Ptolemy had already accepted the Pythagorean opinion that the earth was globular in shape, and based his geographical calculations on this assumption. He also worked out tables of the movement of the planets against the background of the stars, establishing a model of the universe that was accepted and utilized by astronomers and philosophers until Copernicus introduced his cosmological revolution in 1542 and Galileo, with his telescope, confirmed its truth in 1615.

The point in bringing all this up is to illustrate the relativity of all theological understandings because of the major shifts they are subject to due to the changes in our world-view. Back in Section A of Chapter 3 we saw how profoundly the Copernican revolution affected the religious beliefs of Baruch Spinoza, causing him to be expelled from his synagogue, to translate his Hebrew first name to Benedict, and exchange his concept of God entirely from what seemed to him to be the capricious God of the Old Testament to the divine intellect that had established and largely become identified with the laws of nature. We also saw how Albert Einstein had also become alienated from the God of the Bible and had endorsed Spinoza's ideas about God, but having convinced himself that Spinoza's God eliminated any human responsibilities for evil, subsequently suffered very much conflict over the genocide that had been unleashed by Hitler and his followers against the Jewish people.

But we also saw, in Section B of Chapter 3, how the mathematician A. N. Whitehead, born in the midst of the Darwinian Revolution, became eventually a philosopher of the evolution of everything, including of God himself. In the remainder of this chapter we will be exploring the implications of this new scientific and philosophical — and eventually, theological — revolution, particularly for Christianity.

The Christ of the Future

A: God within Process

We need not repeat the collection of quotations (in Chapter 3, Section B) concerning the evolving nature of God in Whitehead's great 1927-28 masterwork, *Process and Reality*, in order to find out what Whitehead thought about God. However, we probably need to know how much his concept of God differed from our usual impressions, formed as much by an overlay of Greek philosophical ideas, as compared to what some very traditional Jews have thought about God as they interpreted the Bible. So perhaps we should take a few samples from a chapter of an anthology covering various religious perspectives on "Process Theology."[1] In the first chapter, "A Jewish Perspective: Divine Power and Responsiveness," Rabbi Bradley Shavit Artson writes:

> God for process thinking is the ground of novelty. God is the fact that a universe established through fixed, changeless laws, still generates novelty all the time; new unprecedented things that did not previously exist. And in process thinking, God shares the experiences of all creatures, and is experienced by all creatures.[2]

And then quoting from a Jewish sage from long ago, Rabbi Moshe Cordovero, Artson continues:

> The essence of divinity is found in every single thing — nothing but it exists. Since it causes every thing to be, no thing can live by anything else. It enlivens them; its existence exists in every existent...Do not say, 'This is a stone and not God.' God forbid! Rather all existence is God, and the stone is a thing pervaded by divinity.[3]

While the above passage may seem extreme in some ways, even to Jews who are not into Kabbalic mysticism, its congruity with the Platonist tradition is unmistakable. Thus we hear again echoes of Plotinus who believed that God is not just everywhere, but that "God is the everywhere in which all things have their existence."[4] It is also reminiscent of the spirituality of St. Francis of Assisi. It is no wonder then, that the theologically inclined followers of Whitehead, have coined the term *panentheism* — everything existing *in* God, and God's creative presence *in* everything! God is not just in a covenant with his chosen people. God has made a covenant or partnership with all of creation.

Especially of note is Rabbi Artson's take on God's power and the problem of evil. But to put Artson's remarks about the part that human choice plays in that matter into a larger context, it might be best to ponder two quotes that Artson again has lifted from largely forgotten Jewish sources. One is from a Hasidic rabbi from 19th century Poland:

> God created the world in a state of beginning. The universe is always in an uncompleted state, in the form of its beginning. It is not like a vessel at which the master works to finish it: it requires continuous labor and renewal by creative forces. Should these cease for only a second, the universe would return to primeval chaos.[5]

And the other, from the same period in Russia:

> The activating force of the Creator must continuously be present within the created object, to give it life and continued existence... And even as regards this physical earth and its inorganic components, their life-force and continued existence is the 'word of God' ...There is a kind of soul and spiritual life-force even in inorganic matter such as stone and dust and water.[6]

The Christ of the Future

Not that these Hasidic rabbis were unknown scientific geniuses, but the first gives us a description of a universe that is in a continual state of evolution, while the second gives a picture that is not unlike that that of the evolutionary philosopher Henri Bergson with his postulation of a *élan vital* or vital force giving a direction (or as Whitehead put it, an "initial aim") to the thrust of creative evolution. Bergson's most famous work, *L'Evolution creatrice*, was first published in 1907 and had a great influence on the thinking of Whitehead, William James, and Teilhard de Chardin — among many others. In 1927, Bergson was awarded the Nobel Prize for literature, even though the Vatican predictably denounced Bergson's book as "pantheistic."

Unlike the clock-like workings of the universe that Newton analyzed and Spinoza theologized, and that Einstein believed in, Bergson had already intuited what we now know — that, at its heart, the universe is like a seething cauldron of quantum energy, the behavior of which is largely unpredictable.

Given all this, what implications does it have for our understanding of evil? One of them, which we've already seen in Chapter 2, Section D, is that, from an evolutionary standpoint, the basic randomness or quantum fluctuations are fundamental to the workings of the evolutionary process, without which eventually life, from it simplest form to its most complex forms, including creatures like ourselves, could not have developed. True, from among all this randomness and chance, nature also plays a role in selection, or as the old slogan goes, "the survival of the fittest" — whether it be the fittest individuals, the fittest species, or the fittest, or the most selfish, genes. But one way or another, some mutations of whatever has emerged are an essential part of the process. And if so, there are bound to be evolutionary accidents, even seeming catastrophes. Contrary to what Einstein kept insisting, God does seem to play dice, not just after all, but from the very beginning.

So then what is the role of humans and the choices they make? Rabbi Artson writes: "One key shift for process thinking, is that God does not exercise coercive power; God exercises persuasive power..." Why? It is because God "lures" us on from within toward fulfilling what Whitehead called the "initial aim" or goal that God has had in mind from the beginning, but leaves us free to cooperate or not. This "initial aim" or "subjective aim" is frequently mentioned in Whitehead's *Process and Reality,* and is described as "a direct derivate from God's primordial nature"[7] and by which "an originality in the temporal world is conditioned, though not determined, by an initial subjective aim supplied by the ground of all order and of all originality."[8] Thus Artson went on to add:

> We know what the initial aim is; we know it intuitively because we prehend it. We do not have to be told: We are each connected to all, and to the creative-responsive love that is God. So we intuit the lure from the inside. Sometimes we choose not to make the right choice, or to do the right thing because of the other powers that impinge upon us: our physicality, drives, selfishness, desires, or laziness. A wide diversity of excuses accounts for our subjective aim perverting God's initial aim which leaves God in covenant, hence vulnerable... Here again we meet a dynamic, relating God who suffers, who becomes vulnerable in having created us.[9]

The question, however, it to what extent we really do intuit or "prehend" (Whitehead's term for a felt relationship or connection between a subject and an object, but which is not necessarily conscious) this "initial aim" of God or purpose?

The Christ of the Future

Augustine famously wrote in the Prologue of his *Confessions*: "Our hearts are made for you, O God, and they will not rest until they rest in you." But how often or how much of the time are we conscious of this? Has there not been, in the biblical tradition, a long history of prophets sent by God precisely to try to correct this amnesia, or what Whitehead called "negative prehensions"?

But as the early scientist and fervently Catholic Blaise Pascal (1623-1662) eventually discovered, and inscribed in his *Memorial*, "the God of Abraham, the God of Isaac, and the God of Jacob," is also "the God of Jesus." So if an evolutionary view of all reality, once relieved of its overburden of Greek philosophy, can be absorbed by Judaism, the question for Christians is whether or not the same can be done for Christianity — and if so, what might be the precise role of Jesus Christ?

B: Teilhard and the Cosmic Christ

The Catholic process theologian Joseph A. Bracken, S.J., in his contribution to this same anthology, has pointed out that Whitehead was not a theologian and only mentions Jesus or Christ in passing.[10] But Bracken, following a lead suggested by another Catholic process theologian, Bernard Lee, suggests that Jesus, because of his own loving response to the God he called "Father," himself became a "lure" drawing us in his own footsteps on the path to union with God. Thus, as Bracken explains it:

> What made Jesus different from other human beings in their reception of a divine initial aim at each moment of their lives is that Jesus realized better than others that it was an inspiration directly from God and responded to what God wanted of him at that moment. As a result, Jesus' sense of self-identity at every

moment of his life was constituted by his conformity to the Father's will for him at that same moment. Thus, he could speak to his contemporaries with the authority of God in a way that no one else, not even the Hebrew Prophets, could claim.[11]

The above is a very good picture, from a Whiteheadian process standpoint, of a "Low Christology," with the human Jesus living his whole life in terms of an ascent to God. But then Bracken moves on to focus on what might be an outstanding example of a "High Christology" in its most modern form, the promotion of a vision of the "Cosmic Christ" by the French Jesuit and priest-paleontologist, Pierre Teilhard de Chardin (1881-1955). Rather than focusing on Whitehead's "brief Galilean vision of humility [which] flickered throughout the ages, uncertainly,"[12] Teilhard would have us focus all our attention on the glorified Christ who, as he described him in the Epilogue of his most widely-read book "invests himself organically with the very majesty of his creation."[13]

It almost seems that, alone in recent times, it was Teilhard who paid much attention to this traditional line of thought passed down from the New Testament and early Christianity. However, even for him, it wasn't easy to maintain his beliefs in view of the expanding field of modern science. And even today, among those who revere Teilhard's thought, and especially his efforts to reconcile faith and science, there remains some skepticism regarding what some refer to as his "Christocentric mysticism." Accordingly, we must examine the reasons for Teilhard's life-long concern.

For one, there was the whole and increasingly difficult problem of maintaining belief in the traditional understanding of Christ as redeemer, indeed, even of our need for redemption. Not that we are innocent of sin — in fact, given the population explosion, we might say that the more people there are, the more sin there is.

But as a scientist well versed in evolutionary thinking, Teilhard knew very well that the tracing of all humanity's problems to an original sin as described in the Book of Genesis was no longer a credible story and that if there was anything like a "fall" at all, it might have to be seen as God's compromising of his divine isolation through sharing his being with creatures. So in 1922, while teaching at the Institut Catholique in Paris, he wrote a confidential essay on the topic.[14] But it fell into the wrong hands and he soon found himself banned from teaching and was eventually sent to do paleontological research in China and forbidden to write anything more that dealt with anything touching Catholic doctrine.

Nevertheless, during his long exile in China, Teilhard continued to think, and to write, this time making sure that his essays — which he sent to his secretary in Paris to be typed and mimeographed — did not fall into the wrong hands. Among those in China who took favorable notice of what Teilhard was doing was a Franciscan missionary and biblical scholar, Gabriel Allegra, who discussed some of these issues with him.[15] Allegra noted that the great medieval Franciscan theologian, John Duns Scotus, had also had problems with the idea that the reason that the Incarnation had taken place was due solely to an original sin by Adam and Eve. Thus Allegra encouraged Teilhard in his views which, like those of the ancient Church theologians, particularly in the East, had focused more on the idea of Christ as coming as a completion or fulfillment of all of creation. Actually, Thomas Aquinas also half admitted the same.[16] The difference between them was that Aquinas listed such a completion of creation as an additional reason for the Incarnation, while Scotus claimed that it would have taken place even if there had been no sin to begin with.

However, the problem that faced Teilhard was more than just that surrounding the doctrine of an original sin. Although Teilhard's chosen profession was as a paleontologist, finding and identifying the relics of earlier forms of life, his specialty was relating these fossils to their geological environment, mainly in the attempt to date them. Accordingly, he had also to keep himself well-informed on developments in planetary and astronomical science. And, as we've already seen (in Chapter 2) certainly the most startling among these latter developments were the findings of Edmund Hubble that took place at the observatory on Mount Wilson near Pasadena, California, during the 1920s.

What Hubble was able to discover with the then new 100-inch diameter Hooker Telescope was that many of the various nebulae or cloudy objects in the night sky were indeed other galaxies, somewhat similar to but separate from our own Milky Way. Up to that time these had only been speculated to exist by a few other thinkers such as the philosopher Immanuel Kant who began to speak about "island universes" as far back as 1755. Likewise, the astronomer William Herschel, in the early 19th century, was convinced that this was indeed the case. Not only that, Hubble, by using spectrographic analyses of the light emitted by these other galaxies, concluded that at least most of them, excepting a few of those closest to us, like the famous M-32 "Andromeda Galaxy," are racing away from us at tremendous speed. Although Einstein had read a paper written by the Belgian cleric and mathematician, Georges Lemaître, in 1927, that suggested the universe had begun with what Lemaître called "a primal atom" and had met Lemaître at the Solvay Conference held in Brussels in 1929, it was only after visiting

The Christ of the Future

with Hubble at the observatory on Mount Wilson in 1931 that Einstein had begun to finally admit that Lemaitre's idea was probably correct. Thus Einstein was forced to revise his own relativistic calculations, and — as we've already seen — eventually had to admit that his insertion of a "cosmological constant" to account for the universe not having collapsed long ago due to the forces of gravity, had been the biggest blunder of his life.[17]

Teilhard's writings after this period reflect many of these developments as well as a great deal of caution regarding the origins of life.[18] In fact, it is safe to say that in his mind "the possible appearance" of "other thinking planets" elsewhere in the universe was seen as something with which Christianity must reckon.[19] Indeed, what was seen by Teilhard as a possibility a few years earlier, had become by 1953, at least in his own mind, all the more probable. Thus he wrote in his essay or note titled "A Sequel to the Problem of Human Origins: The Plurality of Inhabited Worlds":

> No doubt (as happened at the end of geocentrism) it is inevitable that the end of 'monogenism' may well oblige us to revise a good many of out theological 'representations' and make them more flexible...[20]

And just to make sure he was not misunderstood — as he had been in some of his earlier writing when he touched on the subject of *monogenism* — he later attached two footnotes to that word in the same essay; the first explaining that by the term he meant belief in the origins of the human race having been in a single couple and the second suggesting that perhaps 'geo-monism' might be a better word to use.

The parallel Teilhard drew between what the impact of the discovery of intelligent life elsewhere in the universe might

Einstein and the Image of God

mean for Christianity and the impact that the Copernican revolution had on human thinking is apt but perhaps even a bit understated. After all, despite the ecclesiastical furor over Galileo's stubborn efforts to prove that Copernicus was correct and his eventual success in doing so, Christians eventually adjusted to the idea that the Earth no longer was situated at the physical center of the universe, without losing their faith that Jesus had come to save us all. At the very least, most Christians learned from that experience to take the words of the Bible less literally. In fact, Teilhard, to take the best possible view of this prospect, went on to say:

> ... but these adjustments matter little provided that, ever more structurally and dynamically coherent with all we are now discovering in connection with cosmogenesis, one thing remains solidly established: the dogma which sums up all dogmas: 'in Eo Omnia Constant.'[21]

This last quotation above is from verse 17 of the Latin translation of the famous "hymn" found in the first chapter of the Epistle to the Colossians, verses 15-20, where in the first three verses, Christ is described in the following words

15 He is the image of the invisible God,
   the firstborn of creation,
16 for in him all things have been created,
   in the heavens and on the earth
   things visible and invisible,
   whether thrones or dominions or rulers or powers —
   all things have been created through him and for him.
17 He himself is before all things,
   and in him all things hold together.

The Christ of the Future

However, what Teilhard considered to be a "dogmatic" assertion is one thing. The big question is to explain how Christ can be understood as fulfilling this function. That this whole passage represents an advance beyond the earlier and most central writings attributed to St. Paul almost goes without saying. Where Paul's major epistles focus on the redemptive role of Christ as a foundation of Christian discipleship and church order, in the letter to the Colossians we find the foundation for all life established, as it were, from the very beginning, in Christ's role in creation. In this we find an echo or more exactly an anticipation, since it was probably written at least a decade or so before, of the prologue of John's gospel.

In his well-named 2006 study, *A Cosmic Leap of Faith*, theologian Vincent A. Pizzuto has exhaustively studied this whole "hymn" in regard to its authorship, structure, and even more importantly, its doctrinal message. Pizzuto sees the whole passage, as well as the whole epistle, as the product of a single author, who was writing to the Christians of Colossae, which had only recently recovered from a devastating earthquake that had occurred about the year 68 or 69. Thus it predates by at least one decade the earliest estimation for the dates of John's gospel.[22] It also was, much like the Epistle to the Ephesians, a kind of "circular letter" — or "encyclical" — intended not just for Colossiae, but to be passed on to other near-by towns like Ephesus and Laodicea in Asia Minor. It was an area that seems to have been a hotbed of syncretistic religious speculation, some that eventually led to what we know as "Christian Gnosticism." When seen in terms of its "chiastic" structure — two parallel themes joined at one crucial point — this "hymn" or loosely poetic composition appears to have been intended as a kind of creed or summary

Einstein and the Image of God

of Christ's role, first in the creation of the universe, and again, in its redemption. Thus, the second part of the hymn:

> 18 He is the head of the body, the church;
> He is the beginning, the first born of the dead,
> So that he might come to have first place in everything.
> 19 For in him all the fullness of God was pleased to dwell,
> 20 and through him God was pleased to reconcile to himself
> all things, whether on earth or in heaven,
> by making peace through the blood of his cross.

If there is a linguistic point of contact between Paul's actual writing and this letter to the Colossians, it is surely most evident in the concept of Christ as "the image of God" — a description used by Paul in his Second Epistle to the Corinthians[23] — and the use of the analogy of Christ being the "head" of the church as his "body." This also is a continuation of the same analogy as found in Second Corinthians[24], that is carried out even further in universal or cosmic terms in the Epistle to the Ephesians, which many other authorities believe was written either by the same author or else by someone who was very close to the author of the Epistle to the Colossians.[25] If there could be any doubt about this connection between the epistles to Colossians and Ephesians, the wording found in verses 20-23 of the first chapter of the latter should dispel all doubts. There, God's power is described as having

> ...raised him [Christ] from the dead and seated him at his [God's] right hand in the heavenly places, far above all rule and authority and power and dominion, and above every name that is named, not only in this age but also in the age to come. And he has put all things under his feet and has made him

head of all things for the church, which is his body, the fullness of him who fills all in all.

In contrast to the body analogy as found in Second Corinthians, which was seen more in terms of the local congregation, in these two later epistles we find that the church is being described in what appears to be universal or cosmic dimensions — echoing, as it were, the phrase "all things" (*ta panta*) found twice along with "before all things" (*pro pantōn*) in Colossians 1:17, and again the reconciliation of "all things" in Colossians 1:20.

Likewise, both the passages that have been quoted from Colossians and Ephesians contain the word *plērōma* — a word that is usually translated as "fullness," but sometimes as "completion," and which is used a total of about seven times within these same epistles. And lest this kind of expansive vocabulary is seen as being peculiar to the author of these epistles but not characteristic of the ideas held by St. Paul himself, we have to consider even more the closing words of Paul's claims regarding the universality of redemption in the First Epistle to the Corinthians. In that epistle Paul speaks of Christ who, "when all things (*ta panta*) are subjected to him, then the Son himself will be subjected to the one who put all things (again, *ta panta*) in subjection under him, so that God may be all in all (*panta en pasin*)."[26] The idea is almost identical to that found in Colossians and Ephesians: only the use of the word *plērōma* is missing.

While Teilhard's understanding of the Pauline concept of the Pleroma — which he confided to a friend might be seen as "Creation in some way 'completing' God"[27] — fits in nicely with Whitehead's concept of the "consequent nature of God," the problem still remains as how exactly to fit Christ into this scheme of things. Or to be more exact, how would the incarnation of the "Word" or "Son of God" on planet Earth be seen as a vital or essential step toward the "completion" of God who, from the panentheistic view, permeates the whole universe?

Among the things that seemed to puzzle the commentators on Teilhard's writings and thought were some fleeting references to what he termed a "third nature" or "cosmic nature" of Christ — a nature distinct from both his human nature and his divine nature as taught by the Council of Chalcedon back in 451. This rather novel — to say the least — idea of a "third nature" in Christ, Teilhard suggested, might be needed to understand how Christ could be the redeemer or function as the decisive element in the future evolution of the universe — what he sometimes referred to as "the Omega" or "Omega Point" to which all things might be drawn to or around which they might coalesce. His thinking seemed to be that if this Omega Point, which is ultimately God, is to in some way function effectively in respect to human beings, or for that matter, any other intelligent beings elsewhere in the universe, this "point" or goal of evolution had to be in some way *visible* in Christ.

C: Cosmological Reconsiderations

Yet the problem remains *how*. Currently astronomers are rapidly discovering thousands of "exo-planets" (planets outside of our own solar system) every year within our own galaxy. However, these planet-detecting observations are limited to stars that are comparatively close to our solar system. But with an estimated 100 to 400 billion — some would guess up to a trillion — stars in the Milky Way and with an estimated 100 to 200 billion other galaxies in the observable universe, presumably each with billions of stars with their accompanying planets, the chances for the occurrence of life elsewhere in the universe are truly astronomical. So how imagine that the incarnation of God in human form on planet earth could be of any significance for intelligent life elsewhere in the universe? Back in 1924 Teilhard had liked to think of the Incarnation as being something like an "inoculation" of the universe.[28] But by the summer of 1953, when the essay we have been considering was written, the possibility of life on other planets had, in Teilhard's mind, become an overwhelming probability. Thus, it had become more and more problematic for Teilhard as to how the Incarnation of God in human form could remain the central message of Christianity. The result was that essay quoted above, although originally dated June 5, 1953, seems to have remained unfinished with two undated notes added afterwards. They concern what is called the "J. M. hypothesis." This hypothesis is described as:

> 'A Christified human noosphere which gradually extends over the world.' Attractive but contrary to the facts: millions of galaxies, now existing . . . already extinct . . . at unattainable distances: even electromagnetically their distance outruns the life of mankind!
>
> The only solution: in the two combined ideas:
>   a. of a convergent universe (= centered)
>   b. of Christ (3rd nature) centre of the universe.[29]

But as if all this was not enough, there are two more editorial notes attached to the previous note, one which describes Christ's cosmic nature, "enabling him to centre all the lives which constitute a pleroma extended to the galaxies," while the other explains that the "J. M. hypothesis" as later refined, would envision prophets on each "thinking planet," thus spreading the good news throughout the whole universe.

Einstein and the Image of God

However, both of these additional notes, as found in the original French language edition for this same essay bear the initials "N.D.E."— a detail not found in the published English translation, apparently indicating these were additions by the editor.[30]

Nevertheless, this does not appear to be the end of the story. Where the essay quoted above was dated June 5, 1953, there exists a note in one of Teilhard's private notebooks[31], dated September 28, 1953, in which Teilhard expressed some doubts as to how to connect the Jesus of history with what he calls "the Real Christ," or the "Trans-Christ," whose influence or power of attraction would reach out to all of the Universe. He wondered if the "historical Jesus" was more or less a "projection" of the Christ who already transcends all time and space, or, instead, be seen as the "launching"[32] — like a rocket or space-ship?— of the Christ whose journey would transverse all space and time; in other words, the Cosmic Christ.

Of course, there are those who will always find such a "cosmic leap of faith" all too much, or are even scandalized by its sweeping claims. Or there are those who do find it plausible that Jesus was the incarnation of God on earth, but who are still puzzled by what has been called "the scandal of particularity" and ask why such a thing should have happened only once and at such a remote time and place within a small nation that had fallen on such hard times.

Thus, what we see here is that same problem or "scandal" is expanded on a truly cosmic scale. This was the problem that Teilhard, ever since Hubble's discoveries, was still wrestling with until his dying day. No matter how doggedly he held on to his Christian convictions and his determination that Christ must be seen both as he "in whom all things hold together" and that "through him God was please to reconcile all things,"[33] the problem still remains. How can this grand vision, first conceived in terms of an ancient Ptolemaic or pre-Copernican cosmology, be extended to embrace the whole universe? Or should it be? After all, even the Nicene Creed, despite its bold proclamation of the divinity of Christ, nevertheless seems have to have limited the scope of the Incarnation by declaring its purpose to have been "for us men and our salvation..." And had not some rather speculative theologians and philosophers, like Origen of Alexandria, and much later, Giordano Bruno, even speculated as to whether or not life elsewhere in the universe, perhaps more intelligent than we, might even need to be redeemed? So why this increased insistence that Jesus Christ be seen as a universal redeemer? Or might not God have had other plans for other worlds — of if need be, for other universes?

Conclusion

We have seen, in a number of ways, how the thought of Whitehead and Teilhard paralleled or even complemented each other. Both grounded their systems of thought on evolution. Both were dissatisfied with the concept of God as absolute "Being" aloof and alone in itself. Instead, both envisioned God as being more in the state of *becoming*, as being "completed" or fulfilled by creation. For Teilhard, this was seen in terms of the "pleroma" as found in the epistles to the Colossians and Ephesians, while for Whitehead this same idea was "the consequent nature of God."

So how did these two most differ? For one, Whitehead, following the line of Bergson's *Creative Evolution*, saw it as a never-ending process, forever generating new and perhaps even higher forms of life. But based on the present projections of the future of the universe (as we saw in Chapter 2, Section B) this scenario of unending evolution, is, in the end, probably

Einstein and the Image of God

not accurate. The nearly "flat universe" may last forever, but in a state where it will no longer support life. Only an appeal to an imagined "multiverse" sprouting new "universes" or a recycling universe or some other such scenario would seem to save evolution from coming to a dead-end.

In contrast, Teilhard, following the inspiration of the gospels and the rest of the New Testament, saw the whole process as leading to a final consummation in God, where in the end, through the Redemption wrought by Christ, death itself will be defeated and "God will become all in all."[34]

In the closing pages of *Process and Reality*, Whitehead lamented what he saw as the distortion of God's image "When the Western world accepted Christianity, Caesar conquered" and three strains of thought emerged: "God in the image of an imperial ruler, God in the image of a personification of moral energy, [and] God in the image of an ultimate philosophical principle." In other words, God fashioned in the image of the divine Caesars, the Hebrew prophets, and Aristotle's "unmoved mover." Yet despite all this, "The brief Galilean vision of humility flickered throughout the ages, uncertainly." It is a vision which "dwells upon the tender elements in the world, which slowly and in quietness operate by love... It does not look to the future; for it finds its own reward in the immediate present."[35]

So even if Whitehead's and Teilhard's concepts of God show striking parallels, their images of Christ differ markedly. Where Whitehead longed for a return to the humble picture of Jesus of Nazareth before Christianity elevated him to being "the image of God," Teilhard's vision of the Cosmic Christ tried to combine all of these elements, into a single image — much like the Rublev-inspired icon of Christ chosen for the cover of this book — tying the beginning of all things (the

The Christ of the Future

Alpha) to the future (the Omega), not just of humanity, but the whole universe.

Yet, when all is said and done, and as we shall see in the concluding chapter, perhaps we will soon, if we haven't already, have reached the point where all images eventually fail in the face of what remains beyond our comprehension.

---

[1] Cobb, John B. Jr., *Religions in the Making*, 2012.
[2] Cobb, 18.
[3] Cobb, 18.
[4] Plotinus, *Enneads*, VI, 8, 16.
[5] Cobb, 18.
[6] Cobb, 18.
[7] Whitehead, A. N. *Process and Reality*, 67.
[8] Whitehead, 108.
[9] Cobb, 13.
[10] Whitehead, 342-43.
[11] Cobb, 42.
[12] Whitehead, 519.
[13] Teilhard de Chardin, *The Phenomenon of Man*, 197. Published in nearly two dozen languages, the Epilogue (for obvious reasons) was reportedly omitted in the first Russian language version published in the Soviet Union.
[14] Teilhard de Chardin, *Christianity & Evolution*, 45-55.
[15] Allegra, Gabriel M. *My Conversations with Teilhard de Chardin on the Primacy of Christ*, 1971.
[16] Aquinas, Thomas. *Compendium of Theology*, Chap. 201.
[17] Issacson, 355-56.
[18] Teilhard de Chardin, *The Phenomenon of Man*, 47-48.
[19] Teilhard de Chardin, *Christianity & Evolution*, 206-07, n.3.
[20] Teilhard, 234-35.
[21] Teilhard, 234-35.
[22] Brown, Fitzmyer, & Murphy, *New Jerome Biblical Commentary*, 61:18.

[23] 2 Cor 4:4.
[24] 2 Cor 12:12-31.
[25] Pizzutto, Vincent. *A Cosmic Leap of Faith*, 26-34,
[26] 1 Cor 15:27-28.
[27] Jan. 18, 1952 letter to François Richaud, Teilhard Archives, Cor. "R," #118.
[28] Teilhard de Chardin, *Science and Christ*, 60-61.
[29] Teilhard de Chardin, *Christianity & Evolution*, 235-36.
[30] *Oeuvres de Teilhard de Chardin*, X, 281-82. In a letter dated April 9, 1953, (*Letters from a Traveler*, 339) Teilhard mentioned having a conversation in New York with the philosopher Jacques Maritain, who in his final 1968 book complained of Teilhard's ideas as being "a reversal of the Christian perspective" and kind of "new Gnosticism." On the other hand, Teilhard's secretary in Paris was Jeanne Mortier. So as to the identity of "J.M." in the note attached to the essay of July we can only guess.
[31] Teilhard de Chardin, *Journal* 20 [8], 23.
[32] The word used in the handwritten note appears to be *declanché*.
[33] Col 1:17, 20.
[34] 1 Cor 15:28.
[35] Whitehead, 519-22.

Part III
Christ and the God beyond God

We are talking about God. What wonder is it that you do not understand? If you do understand, then it is not God.
(St. Augustine)

Chapter 7
Christ and the God beyond Images

In 1768, the outspoken deist and critic of organized religion, François Arouet — more famously known by his pen name "Voltaire" — wrote that "If God did not exist, it would be necessary to invent him."[1] But if this is true about God, might not the same be said of the "Cosmic Christ" promoted by his distant kinsman, Pierre Teilhard de Chardin, nearly two centuries later?[2] If so, might not these parallel observations be seen as confirming Einstein's own insights or intuitions? These are: first, that you need an infinitely superior intelligence to account for the existence and order of the universe, and second, that for the majority of mankind, this rather abstract God of reason has to be in some sense or way personified. For Christianity, this personification of the divine took place, early on, in the figure of Jesus Christ.

It is hard to avoid the impression that this recurring need to personify the indescribable or transcendent is inborn in human nature, no matter how stubbornly prophets denounced it or philosophers may have resisted it. Some years ago, Bede Griffiths, a Benedictine monk from Great Britain, had gone to India where he developed an ecumenical ashram open to Christians, Hindus, Moslems, Buddhists, and God-seekers of any sort. His experience soon convinced him that the supposed polytheism of the bulk of India's population was only an illusion caused by the various depictions of God inherited from India's ethnic and regional diversity, each of which mirrored one or another aspects of nature — all of it stemming from the one God.[3]

So while Gautama (the original Buddha) may have rebelled against all this imagery in his native India and

Einstein and the Image of God

insisted on not even naming the ultimate reality, the majority of his followers (in the various forms of *Mahayana* Buddhism) have gone on to erect statutes of the Buddha wherever his teachings have spread. And where the biblical prohibition against images of any sort or attempt to represent the divine has taken place, we find that — if we can believe the historical books of the Bible — inevitably these prohibitions fail. Even Moses manages to snatch a glimpse of God's glory as it were, from God's "backside,"[4] while later accounts even describe him as one who encountered God "face to face."[5] And where this same prohibition has been repeated, as in Islam, we find the same problem, as it were transferred, to the prophet, where the veneration of Mohammed has eventually reached the point where even picturing him is considered tantamount to blasphemy. And oddly enough, where one might think that Jesus' death on the cross might strengthen Mohammed's insistence that Jesus was not God's Son — that God is one and that there is no other[6]— there is instead, also in the *Qur'an*, a denial that Jesus was crucified, but instead was taken up directly into heaven.[7]

All this points to a major problem. It seems that even while we need a personal connection to God, our philosophical ideas or preconceptions as to what God must be like get in the way of relating in a personal basis with God. Not only that; these same preconceptions interfere, even more, with our attempts to understand how Jesus, whom Christians believe is, for us, the image of God, was, and still is, both truly human *and* divine.

A: Rethinking Christology

If Christology can be defined as the theological exploration of the divine-human identity of Jesus, it would seem that — as it has often been said — that a major part of the problem is the

Christ and the God beyond God

assumption that Christians can know what God is like independently from God's self-revelation through Jesus.

However, it needs to be recognized that perhaps a major part of the problem is also that we have assumed that we have understood human nature correctly to begin with. Indeed, if we take even a quick look back at the early controversies surrounding the identity of Jesus, we can see that most of the arguments assumed a dualistic or Platonist view of human nature, where body and soul are seen distinct entities, with the latter, the soul, considered to be somehow naturally immortal.

Yet nothing could be further from the biblical point of view. The fact is, that despite frequent mention of the *psychē* in the Greek translation of the Hebrew scriptures, and again in the New Testament, the Hebrew language did not even have a word to describe such a spiritual entity. The Hebrew word *nephesh*, which so often has been translated as "soul," actually meant a *living being* — as contrasted to a dead one, or more exactly a *basher*, a mere body. The difference was all in the *ruach*, a word that can be translated as "wind," "breath," or "spirit." Psalm 104, makes this especially clear: "...when you [God] take away their breath, they die and return to their dust. When you send forth your spirit, they are created..."[8] This point of view also explains why, from the biblical point of view, the only possible concept of an afterlife was in terms of a resurrection of the body. Until Greek, especially Platonist, philosophy came along, there was no biblical concept of a soul — as a kind of spiritual entity that can exist independently of the body — to go to heaven, or for that matter, to hell. The only exception to this ancient Hebrew pattern of thinking in the Old Testament is found in the Book of Wisdom, written in Greek about the time of Christ and not generally accepted by Jews.

Einstein and the Image of God

Nevertheless, it seems that very few early Christian theologians really understood this. One of the few exceptions was, oddly enough, one of the earliest, Justin Martyr, who back in the mid-2nd century asserted that Plato had it wrong.[9] But for most early Christian theologians, the idea that Jesus possessed a human "soul," again in the Platonist sense of that term, stood as a kind of barrier to his divine identity. Arius tried to get around this difficulty by equating Christ with the Platonist concept of a "demiurge," a kind of creative power associated with God, while Apollinaris, again drawing on Plato, suggested that the rational part of Jesus' soul had been replaced by God's "Word." Others simply described Jesus in terms of a human body inhabited by God himself — thus paving the way for the monophysite understanding of Christ, if not in theory, at least in practice.

But suppose we rethink the whole matter in evolutionary terms and see our "soul" as something that develops as we grow and mature, gradually acquiring a spiritual dimension that just might be able, when united to God, to survive death. If so, then as Henri de Lubac showed in his landmark work on *The Mystery of the Supernatural*, this radical openness to God, despite the modified Platonism of so many of the early church theologians, was the view that explains the use of an axiom that appeared early on in Christian history[10], and has been often found in one form or another ever since. In its most compact form it is that "God became man that man might become God."

If this axiom sounds too radical or even slightly blasphemous — how can humans "become God"? — we should first remember two things. One is, as Bart Ehrman warned his readers in Chapters 2 and 3 of his study of *How Jesus Became God*, in the thinking of the ancient world there was not a strict division between God and nature. Instead,

Christ and the God beyond God

there were degrees of divinity. Thus, as we saw in Chapter 5 of this book, St. Paul could proclaim Christ's divinity as "Son of God" and "Lord" without making him identical to God the Father, or as he termed him, "The God" (*ho Theos*).

The second element in this claim about humans "becoming God" has to do with escaping or overcoming death. While many may have wanted to believe that the soul is immune from death, still, in the ancient mindset, only the gods were naturally immortal. But as we have it in the Second Epistle of Peter, this is precisely what has been made possible through Christ: that through Christ's share in divine power, and his promises, we "may escape the corruption that is in the world... " and "become participants of the divine nature."[11]

On the other hand, might we not say (although with less precision) that not just humanity through God's gift or grace, but *all* creation is, in a way, predestined or adopted — not in simply having been created by God, but in the sense of its continued existence being dependent on God, that is, by what theologians used to call "divine concurrence"?

Or again, if we go back to considering why anything exists in the first place — the basic philosophical question as to why there is anything rather than nothing — we are brought back to the Augustine's concept of God as "Being," or as some of the medieval theologians described God's primary quality, his "*aseitas*" — that is, the act of being in and of itself. Thus, (as we saw in Chapter 2) God's most basic property is simply *to be* and for anything else to *exist* is to participate or share in God's being.

Consequently, looked at from the divine perspective — if we can presume to do so — God's creating and sustaining role in the universe (divine concurrence) implies that no event in nature, or in our activities, or any imaginable activity of any sort in the universe is accomplished without God's presence. In this sense of divine *immanence*, all that exists is divine. But no matter how holy or complete we become, our lives as individuals are still only derived or dependent on something else. Even when raised by grace or the Holy Spirit to participate in God's life, we at best are "divine" as adopted sons or daughters of God.

However, it is less commonly pointed out that, strictly speaking, the first part of the statement that "God became man" is just as impossible. Only a "man," a human being with all its limitations, can be truly human. Ontologically speaking — which is to say, in the order of being — God as such cannot actually be a human or become one. That would be a metaphysical contradiction in terms. Taking such ontological restrictions seriously, then it would seem that to say, "God became a human" is just as impossible as to say, "Humans can become God." From this point of view, a Christology of descent seems to be as impossible as one of ascent. Nevertheless, in the order of divine concurrence it is possible to say that God descends into humanity, just as surely, and perhaps with much greater certainty than we can say any particular human ascends to divinity or participation in God's life. The reason for this is because God is the altogether necessary precondition or ground of existence. Our existence is entirely contingent on God's being, even if our individual identity, rooted in our physicality, marks each of us as distinct from our creator.

Yet in the case of Jesus, was not only his existence, much as ours, entirely contingent on God, but even more, was not his individual identity as a human in some very unique way identified personally with God's concurrence in human history? If so, then perhaps we come as close as it is possible to saying that God has incarnated himself in a human life. Yet this would be without destroying what it means to be a human being, or, on the other hand, without the primary agent of that concurrence ceasing to be God. In this way, might we not say that not only the degree of the divine in every aspect of the life

Christ and the God beyond God

of the man Jesus, but even more the clarity with which this has been revealed, is how he may have been preeminently different from us?

Strictly speaking, of course, God alone is, or ever can be, God. Divinity, in essence, is incommunicable. Thus Augustine, who also used the "God became man that man might become God" maxim in its original form, qualified it somewhat when on another occasion he paraphrased it to write, "The only Son of God became a son of man to make many men sons of God."[12]

Certainly, this qualification is what one might expect from him who has been called "The Doctor of Grace," and who even explained the status of Jesus as the "Son of God" in terms of his understanding of the predestination of the saints. Thus, in his treatise on the subject of divine predestination, Augustine wrote:

> The grace that makes any man a Christian from the first moment of his coming to believe is the same grace that made this man the Christ from his coming to be a man. The Spirit through whom men are reborn is the same Spirit through whom Christ was born... The predestination of the saints is the same predestination that reached its greatest glory in the Saint above all other saints... [and] He who was to be the son of David in his human nature was to be the Son of God in power through the action of the Spirit of holiness... This unique taking to himself of human nature by God the Word came about in such a way, too mysterious for our understanding, that with truth and accuracy the Word could be called at one and the same time the Son of God and the son of man...[13]

Notice how, in the above passage, Augustine deftly wove together what we have tended to think of as opposites, a "low Christology" which sees the human nature of Jesus being taken up or "predestined" through the power of the Holy Spirit to

Einstein and the Image of God

become the Christ and the "son of God in power," is balanced with a "high Christology" which sees this same action as being the effect of "God the Word" taking to himself a human nature, thus becoming "at one and the same time the Son of God and the son of man." But all this, in turn, leads us back to the doctrine of God as a trinity and its problematic relationship to the conviction that there can be only one God.

B: *Christ and the Triune God*

In his 1989-90 Gifford Lectures, the Catholic theologian and scholar of comparative religion, Raimon Panikkar, went so far as to deny that the strict kind of monotheism that we associate with Judaism and Islam is compatible with the Christian doctrine of the Incarnation.[14] Perhaps this might be expected from a theologian who, although Spanish by nationality — born in Barcelona of a Catalan mother — had a father who was a Hindu. In any case, Panikkar was often was quick to point out that the idea of God being in some sense triune is hardly unique to Christianity. It can be found in the writings of Plato and even more clearly in Hindu thought. It is (as was already noted in Chapter 2 of this book) also incipient in Hebrew thought, with its frequent references to God's *Ruach* or "Spirit" and its personification of God's *Hochmah* or "Wisdom."

This personified Wisdom, in turn, was identified by the Jewish philosopher, Philo of Alexandria, as the equivalent of the Greek concept of the *Logos* as the divine "Reason" or "Word" permeating the universe through the power or spirit of God. So while Bishop Spong's reflection about his not being sure if God is actually a trinity may not be uncontestable, his opinion about the human tendency to think about God in trinitarian terms can be seen as clearly evident.

Might not this tendency be also seen in the process philosophy of A. N. Whitehead, glimpses of which we have

Christ and the God beyond God

already seen (in Chapters 3 and 6). The idea that Jesus was different from other humans in that he lived in complete conformity to what Whitehead called God's "initial aim" would certainly seem to fit in with a "low Christology" that sees Jesus' uniqueness in terms of a difference of *degree* of responsiveness to God's Holy Spirit. On the other hand, would not a view that sees Jesus as the unique embodiment of this same "initial aim" correspond more or less exactly to the "high Christology" that identifies him as God's *Logos* or "Word" who, in the words of John's gospel, "became flesh"? In this latter case, then the difference between Jesus and other humans would be seen not just in terms of degree but in terms of a difference of *kind*. But as we've already seen, the major challenge for Christianity has been trying to keep a balance between these contrasting approaches.

However, might not these two approaches be seen more as complimentary rather than sharply contrasting in respect to each other when considered in terms of their function as images, rather than the substance or essence of what the image represents? For someone like Whitehead, who saw the universe as in an unending evolution, God is a formative agent present in everything that exists, giving it an "initial aim."[15] Thus, for Whitehead, the figure of Jesus of Nazareth, whose message, as Whitehead described it — "dwells upon the tender elements in the world, which slowly and in quietness operate by love" and [whose message] "finds purpose in the present immediacy of a kingdom not of this world," and "does not look to the future" but "finds its own reward in the immediate present"[16] — had a great attraction.

Compare Whitehead's reading of the gospels to that of Teilhard, who chose more to dwell on the mystery of the Incarnation and its implications for a universe that seems, due to Hubble's discoveries in the 1920s, might eventually suffer a cosmic cataclysm, or what has been called a "heat death." Thus, for Teilhard, as we have already seen, the figure of the historical Jesus might be seen as the beginning or "launching" of a Cosmic Christ whose function as "the Alpha and the Omega", (the beginning and the end) must "become co-extensive with the physical expanse of time and space."[17]

It may be debated as to what extent Whitehead considered himself a Christian or his system of thought compatible to Christian orthodoxy. But there is no question as to Teilhard's intention to remain faithful to his Catholic allegiance despite his troubles with the official censors in Rome. Yet for both, the figure of Jesus served as what Whitehead called a "lure," or as he described it "an 'objective lure' for feeling" — one that serves as a kind of conduit "into subjective efficiency."[18] For Whitehead, the historical Jesus was an image or example as to how God's love operates in the world. But for Teilhard, the exalted figure of the Cosmic Christ not only was, but still is, in the words of the Epistle to the Colossians, "the image of the unseen God... in him ... and through him, and for him all things were created ... and in him all things hold together."[19]

Knowing now what we do about the extent of the universe, we can even more appreciate why Teilhard worried as to how these expansive, even extravagant, words from the Epistle to the Colossians might make sense to intelligent life elsewhere on other planets. Would the image of Cosmic Christ make any sense to them or even be recognizable? And what if there turned out to be, after all, other universes? And in that case, would not multiple incarnations make more sense? Or must we not, at this point, recognize that images, however exalted that they may be, are, at best, only images pointing to a still unknown reality?

Christ and the God beyond God

C: The God beyond God

The enigmatic phrase "God beyond God" was first made famous by the 14th century German Dominican Johann Eckhart von Hochheim (1260-1328). Also known as "Meister Eckhart," due to his having been a professor of theology for a time at the University of Paris, he was highly respected — having been given many positions of high responsibility in the Dominican order — as well as a spellbinding preacher and writer. Nevertheless, he seems to have left many of his listeners and readers somewhat confused about the real meaning of his often paradoxical language. Such, for example, was his insistence on making a distinction between God and the "God-head," or, as he is often quoted today, his talk about "the God beyond God," thus making a distinction between the manifestation of God as a Trinity and God's essence; or, perhaps less radically, between our ideas about God and what God actually is.[20]

Another expression of Eckhart that seems to have caused some puzzlement was his repeated references to the "Ground" both of God and the soul— made more popular in recent times by theologian Paul Tillich as the "Ground of Being," — which in turn might seem to imply a distinction between Augustine's definition of God as "Being" and something more still more basic.[21] Yet Eckhart was not content to leave it at that, but went so far as to proclaim that in itself to *exist* is to be God, at least in the sense that, as we've already seen, everything that is, insofar as it exists, partakes in the divine quality of *being* as such. Therefore to exist, at least in some sense, is to already be divine!

Almost needless to say, such language aroused suspicion and confusion among more conservative hearers and eventually led to Eckhart being called up before the Church's Inquisition or committee of doctrinal watchdogs to explain

Einstein and the Image of God

himself. The inquisitors drew up a list of suspected heretical statements compiled from quotations from Eckhart's own writings, which were generally in Latin, and from transcripts of his sermons, which were mostly in German. And the list was a very long one, at first consisting of forty-nine articles, later expanded to fifty-nine.[22]

Aside from all this misunderstanding of what Eckhart was saying — and his own accusations that the inquisitors were too stupid to understand him correctly! — one of the main accusations leveled against Eckhart's thought seemed to be that it appeared, at least to the inquisitors, to be a form of *pantheism*, that is, that everything, and everyone, is, in a sense, God. Certainly, sometimes Eckhart's language, such as his assertion that we all, indeed, everything that exists, shares in God's own being, gives that impression. But Eckhart tried to defend himself, invoking passages from St. Augustine, which he claimed that in effect, say much the same. So again, we can see the important difference between *being* as such or in itself (Augustine's definition or description of God) and *existence*, which implies dependence upon something else in order to be. Thus Eckhart's insistence that everything that exists shares God's being, and that, accordingly, all of us are, in a sense, by nature, divine.

Another major concern the Inquisitors had seems to have centered on suspicions that Eckhart was playing dangerous games with his explanations of the doctrine of God as a trinity. As Eckhart saw it, the Holy Trinity might be described as a "boiling" (*bullatio*) within God's being, while creation is kind of "boiling over" (*ebullatio*) of God's own being. As a result, God, whose essence is hidden from us, is nevertheless perceived as Being (*ens*), and thus, as the source of existence, as "Father," then again as true (*verum*) or Truth, which we call

Christ and the God beyond God

"Son," and finally as good (*bonum*) or Goodness, which we call "Spirit."[23]

But even in this, Eckhart was not the radical innovator that he was accused of being, for much of what he was saying was rooted in the thought of that even more famous Dominican, St. Thomas Aquinas. For example, it was Aquinas who taught that what we call "persons" in God are really distinct "subsistent relations" or activities that, as Joseph Bracken has described it, are "three entities that are themselves only in terms of their ongoing relations to each other."[24] In Eckhart's analogy, it is this internal dynamism of God's being, God's knowing, and God's loving that is likened to a cauldron or kettle that boils over, spilling out, as it were, thus creating the universe.

However use of such analogies to describe the activity of God as a trinity does not exhaust the mystery of God's being or essence — thus Eckhart's appeal to the "God beyond God." In this he also seemed to be following Aquinas who wrote that the ultimate human knowledge about God is one "that knows that it does not know God."[25] Thus, when all is said and done, we can not know, at least in mental or conceptual terms, who or what God really is. All we can know is what God isn't.

This insight is nothing new. In fact, it has a very long history within the Christianity reaching as far back to what is sometimes called the *apophatic* theological tradition — from the Greek *apo* ("aside from" or "outside of") and *phaō* (to speak) — as contrasted to the *kataphatic*, or saying everything that can be said. Its roots are in neo-platonic philosophy, but many see it backed up by the biblical warning that, again, "... no one shall see me [God] and live."[26] The idea was to call into question the human tendency to think or say as much as possible about God, then end up having to admit that all our conceptualizations are woefully inadequate. So why not

Einstein and the Image of God

instead just skip all these futile attempts to reason things out and simply plunge into the abyss of the unknown, purging our mind of all attempts at conceptualization?

The first great Christian exponent of this approach seems to have been, as far as scholars can guess, Severus, the Bishop of Antioch in Syria (d. 538), who tried to pass off his own writings on this subject as having been the work of Dionysius, a convert of St. Paul mentioned in the Acts of the Apostles[27], who apparently was known as having associated himself with the philosophical elite at the Areopagus in Athens. According to "Pseudo-Dionysius," as this writer is now known:

> [T]he most divine knowledge of God, that which comes through unknowing, is achieved in a union which is far beyond mind, when the mind turns away from all things, even from itself.[28]

At first, the Eastern Orthodox or Byzantine Church was very cool to Severus and his writings, as he was suspected of being a monophysite. A century or so later, his reputation was defended by St. Maximus the Confessor (d. 662), an abbot and theologian in Constantinople. Eventually, Latin translations of Severus' works had reached the Western church, which naively took the attribution to Dionysius the Areopagite literally, and in some instances, even confused him with St. Denis, who was believed to have been the first bishop of Paris. In any case, the influence of the Pseudo-Dionysian writings and their apophatic approach became very strong, not just among mystical writers — like the anonymous author of the English spiritual classic, *The Cloud of Unknowning*, or the works of the Spanish master of the spiritual life, St. John of the Cross — but even among some theologians, such as St. Bonaventure. Among the latter, that is, theologians who

Christ and the God beyond God

adopted at least some of the Pseudo-Dionysian ideas, the most enthusiastic was Eckhart, who, despite his Aristotlean-Thomistic intellectual formation, realized that, beyond a certain point, no more can or should be said.

It is important that this principle, indeed fact, be kept in mind, not just in the understanding of Christianity, but ultimately of any of the "higher religions" as they are sometimes called. Certain patterns tend to repeat themselves. One of these is the occurrence of apophatic mysticism and a corresponding approach to theology. After you have described the ultimate or the transcendent in every possible way that you can, you reach the point where you realize that no description is adequate and decide that the best way of honoring or relating to that mystery is to give up and be silent, or simply give quiet testimony by the manner of one's life. This is apparently what Siddartha Gautama, the original Buddha, did, casting aside the whole Hindu pantheon, at the price of being considered a "heretic." But in no way was he an "atheist," at least in the aggressive, anti-theistic sense of that word. At most we might call him a "reverent agnostic" — even if we temper that by considering him a radically religious one.

Today, we can see, in the wake of the truly amazing achievements of modern science, a new reluctance to admit that there is anything about the universe that we can't eventually know or even accomplish. Thus Einstein's admission, as late in his life as 1950, that he remained an "agnostic" when it come to the ultimate mysteries about the universe and God, do not sit well with those who would like to imagine that science and the power of reason can solve all our problems. For as he had cautioned his admirers back in 1937 as war and increasing violence already threatened to engulf the whole world:

Einstein and the Image of God

> Let us not forget that human knowledge and skills alone cannot lead humanity to a happy and dignified life. Humanity has every reason to place the proclaimers of high moral standards and values above the discoverers of objective truth. What humanity owes to personalities like Buddha, Moses, and Jesus ranks for me higher than all the achievements of the inquiring constructive mind.[29]

So am I suggesting that we must do the same as the Buddha did, disposing of all the mythical accretions of Hinduism, equally to Western or Bible-based religion? Maybe, although perhaps not so radically — for after all, we do have the historical example of Jesus of Nazareth and what he believed and instructed us to do and himself did. Can we not at least try to do the same?

Or might we not even see, with the impulse of faith, something more in the line of a "high Christology," with Jesus as being sent to us by God, as God's own image of himself drawn in human terms, one in which God reveals himself, as Whitehead put it, as "our fellow sufferer"?[30] Or might not we, with Teilhard's celebrated optimism, take that vision even one step farther, and see him as Teilhard saw him, as the focal point of the *Pleroma* — "the grand completion (at once quantitative and qualitative) of the universe in God"?[31]

D: Hope and Faith beyond Beliefs

Having come to this last point, where having reached what seems to be the very limits of faith, we find ourselves in the puzzling conundrum of having to admit that the highest knowledge is to be found what Nicolas of Cusa called "learned ignorance" — the realization of knowing that, when all is said and done, we know relatively little. So we may well

Christ and the God beyond God

ask, "What is the point of having faith to begin with? Why believe in anything at all?"

Such questions, however, overlook several important facts about life, as well as the importance of faith and, perhaps even more fundamentally, the importance of hope. As the late first or early second century Christian treatise known as the "Epistle of Barnabas" put it, of the three main teachings that Christ left us, the first and most basic is "the hope of life, [which is] the beginning and end of faith."[32] One must, I think, take it for granted that the author was talking about the hope of eternal life. If Christianity could not have offered that hope, I doubt very much that it would have survived the death of Jesus on the cross. Nor can one possibly imagine the willing deaths of the apostles and the thousands upon thousands of Christian martyrs who followed in their footsteps as having been inspired by a hopelessly lost cause.

The astounding growth of Christianity against all odds during the first three centuries that it remained proscribed and persecuted seems only to have been possible because it followers believed that Jesus, through his resurrection from the dead, had actually overcome death and thus gsve hope to his followers that they might do the same. As St. Paul put it to the Corinthians in his reversed but dazzling logic, "If there is no resurrection of the dead, then Christ has not been raised; and if Christ has not been raised, then our proclamation has been in vain and your faith has been in vain." And in that case "If for this life only we have hoped in Christ, we are of all people the most to be pitied."[33] In other words, even if we allow that Paul's idea of resurrection was something a lot more spiritual than bodies jumping up out of graves[34], still, it seems Paul thought that without the hope of life after death, Christians are poor, hopeless, fools.

Einstein and the Image of God

I think, however, that we need not go quite such extreme lengths to make the same point. If, according to a literal translation of the statement found in the Epistle to the Hebrews, "Faith is the reality (*hypostasis* or 'substance') of things hoped for, the proof (*elegos* or 'assurance') of things unseen …"[35], then it would seem logical to assume that the stronger our faith the more assured or certain our convictions or beliefs. But as we saw, in the concluding paragraph of section C in Chapter 1, experience, especially the experience of the mystics and saints down through the ages has shown otherwise. It appears that the more deeply faith is rooted, the more inadequate the ideas or beliefs associated with it become. This was also the finding of the theologian and religious psychologist James W. Fowler and his analysis in his 1981 study titled *The Stages of Faith*.

It is this same phenomenon that seems to have motivated another theologian, Wilfred Cantwell Smith, to write his 1979 book, *Faith and Belief*. Despite their equivocation in everyday language, Smith insisted that they are, in fact, two different, although commonly associated, things. *Faith*, in the sense that the Greek word *pistis* is used in the Gospels, is primarily a loving trust in God or in those believed to have been sent by God. *Belief*, on the other hand, generally means quite something else: it means a deeply or firmly held conviction, often one for which the evidence is not obviously present. Yet, with its Germanic roots (*lieb* meaning "love") belief is obviously connected to faith as a form of loving trust, thus faith is more a matter of the "heart" (*leib*). In contrast, belief is more a matter of the "head" — or as we might even put it today, "a head-trip." Thus, if theology is faith seeking understanding, as I have tried to illustrate in a number of ways in this book, religious doubt or confusion is almost inevitable whenever our understanding of the world around

Christ and the God beyond God

us changes. This is because the beliefs in which our faith is expressed are formulated in terms of our world-view when that world-view changes — as when Copernicus displaced Earth from the center of the universe, or Darwin uncovered our evolutionary past among the primates. Should we then be surprised that if the ancient beliefs and the way our speech still reflects them — even the idea that the sun circles the earth, thus "rises" and "sets" — cannot be taken literally any more? And if this is the case with much of our everyday language, should we be surprised if the language of faith, expressed in similar beliefs, is affected the same way?

Now, if the above is true in terms of the average or popular level of understanding, how much more so can it not be so in the process of growth and maturation of the person who seriously pursues union with God? Not only that, must not we expect that as faith, as a truly loving trust, increases, the reliance on belief or doctrines must also diminish? After all, does not the true lover, if he or she truly loves, depend less and less on the outward expressions or assurances of love?

The same rule applies to any hopes for a heavenly reward. In those who seek God above all, self-centered hopes and dreams must eventually give way more and more to unselfish acceptance of whatever God wills. St. Paul, in his avowed willingness to be himself "lost" if through that loss his own people could be saved[36] may seem excessive, but it is not unique among the saints. In fact, all the masters of spirituality, ranging from the Buddha to John of the Cross, have taught much the same.

So should we be surprised then, that the seekers after God, if they are truly seeking God, will be eventually deprived of all the helps and consolations, the various tokens, assurances and promises that lured them on in the beginning stages of their journey to God?

Einstein and the Image of God

So it is with our various images of God, including Jesus Christ himself. In his homily or commentary on the feast of the Ascension, St. Leo the Great — the pope who wrote the decisive letter to the bishops meeting at Chalcedon in the year 451 — described how, in Christian minds, the ascended Christ

> ... now began to be more indescribably more present in his divinity to those from whom he was further removed in his humanity. A more mature faith enabled their minds to stretch upward to the Son in his equality with the Father; it no longer needed contact with Christ's tangible body, in which as man he is inferior to the Father. For while his glorified body retained the same nature, the faith of those who believed in him was now summoned to the heights where, as the Father's equal, the only-begotten Son is reached not by physical handling but by spiritual discernment.[37]

Of course, a cynic may point out that Pope Leo's reasoning only repeats the ancient pattern of the exaltation, glorification, and even deification, of dead heroes. But in doing that, one may be also missing the whole logic of the Christian emphasis on the Incarnation — the belief that God has, in very personal way, entered into his creation, with all that it entails, including undergoing death. Even more, this *kenosis*, or self-emptying not only involved God's accommodation to the limitations of human reasoning, such as found in Jesus' use of parables, but even going so far as to conform to the ancient human concept of expiation or atonement through sacrificial death — as found depicted in the "Suffering Servant" passages of the Book of Isaiah the Prophet.[38]

Likewise, one may also object that Pope Leo's sermon was full of its own mythic images, including those drawn by St. Luke when he depicted the scene described in his gospel[39] and

Christ and the God beyond God

in his Acts of the Apostles with its accompaniment of angels and clouds.[40] But if one is going to object to all this, one must object to almost all human language, which, except for grunts or groans, is fundamentally analogical in nature, the analogies and metaphors drawn mostly from mental pictures. Think of first alphabets or even the ideograms that preceded them, and try to imagine communication without them. Can some kind of image of God, even if one is capable of thinking as abstractly as an Einstein, ever be completely absent from the reflective and probing mind?

In this case, then might not Christians also rethink Einstein's classification of what he saw as the three levels or stages of religion in terms of the images that they evoke — perhaps in terms of Christ as prophet, priest, and king? First mentioned by Eusebius of Caesarea and much later developed at length by the reformer Jean Calvin, perhaps these offices or functions of Christ should be rearranged in the order suggested by Einstein's levels or stages of religion.

If so, then, at the most basic level, that of a religion of fear, which as Einstein noted, tends in time to be characterized by the formation of "a special priestly caste which sets itself up as a mediator between the people and the beings they fear..."[41] Thus we have image of Christ on the cross, offering his life as an atonement for mankind's sins, lest we ourselves suffer our well-deserved punishment. Thus we have, early on in Christianity, the image of Christ as the new "High Priest," as found especially in the Epistle to the Hebrews.[42]

Next, we have the picture of Christ with which both Einstein, as well as Whitehead, were more comfortable, that of Christ as teacher or "Prophet." But this latter term must not be so much understood in the narrow sense of a foreteller of the future, but in its original sense of someone who speaks for God, thus, as advancing what Einstein saw as the second stage

Einstein and the Image of God

or level of religion — the evolution of humanity's moral or ethical sensibilities.

Finally, we have the image of Christ as "King," which back in 1940 Teilhard saw as part of the "irresistible advance of the Christian consciousness toward a more universal and realistic appreciation of the Incarnation" ... and which image, as he went on to explain "for us, fascinated by the newly uncovered magnitude of the universe, it expresses exactly that aspect of the God which is needed to satisfy our capacity for worship."[43] Yet even here Teilhard expressed some caution, as he went on to say:

> Between Christ the King and the Universal Christ, there is perhaps no more than a slight difference of emphasis, but it is nevertheless all-important. It is the whole difference between an external power, which can only be juridical and static, and an internal domination which, inchoate in matter and culminating in grace, operates upon us by and through all the organic linkages of the progressing world.[44]

Yes, it does make difference, because as has been emphasized, one way or another, in this book, our beliefs and theology are largely expressed in terms of our cosmology or world-views and these latter have gone through revolutionary changes — be it the Copernican revolution, the Darwinian revolution, or even that of "Einsteinian" relativity — since Christianity first began. If then, this is the case, the challenge is to choose our images carefully, and to do so, not so much with an eye to the past, however important that may have been, but with an eye on the future in our on-going quest for the still largely "unknown God."

Christ and the God beyond God

[1] Moland, *Oeuvres de Voltaire*, Vol 10, 402-05.
[2] Mortier & Auboux, *A Teilhard Album*, 8.
[3] Griffiths, Bede. *The Cosmic Revelation*, 1983.
[4] Exod 33:18-23.
[5] Deut 34:10.
[6] Surah 5:72-73.
[7] Surah 4:157-58.
[8] Ps 104:29-30.
[9] Justin Martyr, *Dialogue with Trypho*, Chapters 5-6.
[10] Irenaeus, *Adversus heresies*, Book III, Chap. XIX.
[11] 2 Pet 1:3-4.
[12] Augustine, *Sermo* 194.
[13] Augustine, *On the Predestination of the Saints*, Chap. 15, 30-31.
[14] Panikkar, *The Rhythm of Being*, Lecture V, Part C.
[15] Whitehead, A. N., *Process & Reality*, 67, 108.
[16] Ibid., 580.
[17] Teilhard de Chardin, *Human Energy*, 91.
[18] Whitehead, Ibid., 133.
[19] Col 1:1-17.
[20] Colledge, Edmund & McGinn, Bernard, *Meister Eckhart, The Essential Sermons, Commentaries, Treatises, and Defense*, 35-37.
[21] McGinn, Bernard, *Meister Eckhart: Teacher and Preacher*, 402.
[22] Colledge & McGinn, 71-72.
[23] Ibid., 35, 302, n63.
[24] Bracken, Joseph A. *The World in the Trinity*, 8.
[25] Aquinas, Thomas, *Summa Theologica*, I, a3; *Contra Gentiles*, I, 5.
[26] Exod 33:20.
[27] Acts 17:34.
[28] Luibheid & Rorem, *Pseudo-Dionysius: The Complete Works*, 109.
[29] Calaprice, *The Ultimate Quotable Einstein*, 445.
[30] Whitehead, *Process & Reality*, 532.
[31] Teilhard, *Toward the Future*, 97.
[32] Barn 1:6.
[33] 1 Cor 15: 13-14,19.
[34] 1 Cor 15:35-55.

[35] Heb 11:1.
[36] Rom 9:3.
[37] *Patres Latines*, 54: 397-399.
[38] Is 42:1-7; 49:1-7; 50:4-9; 52:13-53:12.
[39] Luke 24:50-53.
[40] Acts 1:6-11.
[41] Einstein, *Ideas and Opinions*, 24.
[42] Cf. Hebrews chapters 3-5.
[43] Teilhard de Chardin, *Toward the Future*, 98-99. The feast of Christ the King had been instituted by Pope Pius XI in 1929 as countermeasure to growing nationalism, and the various totalitarianisms that followed in its wake. More recently, this commemoration has been adopted by many other (Anglican, Episcopal, Lutheran, Methodist, etc.) "main-line" churches in turn.
[44] Ibid., 99.

Some Concluding Afterthoughts

While this book might be seen as a kind of personal *summa theologica*, it is not in the sense of a massive summary of all possible questions and answers about God in the manner of the medieval theologians like Thomas Aquinas. Instead, it is, in a rather personal way, as I reach the final chapter of my life, a summary of my own views, as a theologian raised in the Catholic faith, about God and about the Christ who is described in the New Testament as "the image of God," "the image of the invisible God" and as "the exact imprint of God's very being."[1] However, the path to this conclusion has been for me, a very long and sometimes troubled one, one that involved at least two distinct crises of faith.

The first took place nearly fifty years ago, when in the midst of a vocational crisis, my faith in God was severely shaken, even to the point that I began to despair for my life. Although the initial trauma itself soon passed with the help of what I really do believe was the grace of God, I spent a major part of the following year in a desert retreat in Arizona attempting to reconstruct my belief system before reaching a decision to pursue post-gradate studies in philosophy and theology, which ended up taking place at the University of Ottawa and St. Paul University, closely allied institutions located in Canada's capital city.

However, during that initial winter in Arizona, there was one book that particularly influenced my thought. It was titled *The Lord of the Absurd*, and if anything, it shook my faith even more — even to the point where I had to start all over again, as they say, "from scratch." It had been written by someone whom I greatly admired, or even envied at the time, a Dominican priest-scholar from my own state of Michigan, Fr.

Einstein and the Image of God

Raymond Nogar. Following in the tradition of his religious order's great saint and scholar, Thomas Aquinas, Nogar had written a weighty book titled *The Wisdom of Evolution*, using Teilhard de Chardin's evolutionary vision as a background framework, much as Aquinas had used Aristotle's physics and metaphysics, to produce a synthesis between science and faith. Imagine my renewed despair when this latest and last book of Nogar's (he died suddenly in 1967 at age 51) seemed to repudiate everything he'd written before.[2]

But then, as I pondered this last, and to me devastating, book of Nogar's, it gradually began to dawn on me that what Nogar had done, among other things, was to reverse much of the reasoning in what Aquinas had attempted to do in his famous demonstrations — often mistakenly presented as "proofs" of God's "existence" — instead of as to how people come to a belief in God. Instead of using Aristotle's presentation of the four causes (material, efficient, formal, and final) as the basis of cosmological arguments in favor of there being a God, Nogar had shown, at least to my mind, that without there being a God, it is impossible to make any sense out of the chaos, disorders, and tragedies that characterize the evolution of the Universe at large. In other words, I came to the conclusion that Nogar had experienced and passed through his own existential crisis of faith. And if that had been the case, so could I.

Imagine my surprise when, a year later, as I began my further studies in Ottawa, the among the first philosophy courses I was advised to take was one on "Philosophical Problems in Evolution," taught by a former pupil of Nogar. This young professor, although he raised plenty of problems, personally tried to convince me that Nogar had not gone through a crisis of faith. But, of course, at that time, having gone through my own personal crisis, I didn't believe him.

Afterthoughts

But it was only a few years later, when I was studying Teilhard's private "journals" or notebooks from the latter part of his life at the Jesuit archives near Paris that I found an entry dated July 15, 1954, just short of nine months before his death. It reads (in part) that God is "indemonstrable" but instead amounts to *"L'Exigence Existentielle,"* the existential demand for an irreversible totalization, thus with the requirement that "everything" in some way or another survives "forever."[3] I wonder now if Nogar had somehow seen the same journal note. Or had he himself been thinking along the same lines before he died?[4]

My second great crisis of faith, however, was not about God but about Christ. And it occurred not as a result of scholarly arguments but as the result of a long-delayed trip to and four months stay in the Holy Land back in the winter and into the spring of 1980. After about eight years of teaching, I had signed up for a semester of additional post-graduate study at the Ecumenical Institute for Advanced Theological Studies located about half-way between Jerusalem and Bethlehem, almost literally a stone's throw distance from the "Green Line" separating the State of Israel from the occupied Palestinian "West Bank."

There I found myself in what was, for me, a truly alien world, wondering what most inhabitants of that world — overwhelmingly Jewish on one side, and now mostly Muslim on the other — could ever make of my own beliefs in the divinity of Christ or God as a "Holy Trinity," or even more, of Teilhard's concept of a "Cosmic Christ." In other words, in my mind, the earthly reality of Jesus of Nazareth, the "Historical Jesus" had collided headlong with the exalted doctrines of the "Christ of Faith." The icon or image (the same as on this book's cover which I had treasured in my mind

Einstein and the Image of God

since my grad-school years) had become a test of faith. It was this double collision between faith and skepticism that I hoped to resolve by writing this book.

Thus, with the conclusion of the last chapter, I think we have come more or less through a full circle. Having begun with a God who is a mystery or the great unknown at the heart of the universe, we find ourselves ending with a God who still remains the great unknown. So have we really learned anything worthwhile in all this effort?

It seems to me, that in the end, especially if we have lived long enough (I'm now about half-way through my eighty-third year) — or if we have unexpectedly matured some years before that — we all end up, to some degree or in one form or another, as agnostics. Or if that term, with all its baggage, sounds too harsh or too negative, we become adepts of that school of "learned ignorance" that the great 15th century scholar and churchman, Nicholas of Cusa, once wrote about. We end up knowing that in the end we know that we do not know, and aside from that, we have learned very little indeed.

However, it also seems to me that such agnosticism can assume three forms. The first is that reverent agnosticism of the mystics or of others who — like Cusa — realize that, when all is said and done, we know very little in comparison to what must lie beyond. Or if we were to take this reverent agnosticism to its most extreme degree, we end up, like the Buddha, refraining from trying to speak of or name this great unknown at all.

The second form of agnosticism, as I see it, is that scornful or irreverent agnosticism that is often associated or even confused with atheism in the popular mind. Indeed, one might devoutly wish that a few more of the "new atheists" that we have seen in this study had the humility to be genuine agnostics, or at least recognize the logical truth of the saying

Afterthoughts

that "the absence of evidence does not constitute the evidence of absence" — especially when the topic in question is God.

Which in turn leads us to the third and most consistent or thorough-going form of agnosticism, that shown by Einstein, especially toward the end of his life when, as quoted in the introduction to this book, he admitted that when all is said and done, not only in regard to our knowledge of God but of the universe itself, we really know comparatively little: that deepest mysteries remain unsolvable, or as he put it: "The real nature of things, that we shall never know, never." [5]

However, this last remark of Einstein brings up, to my way of thinking, in all three of these forms of agnosticism, there remains a residue of belief, other than one's personal conviction that his or her form of agnosticism is best — at least for themselves.

For example, the reverent form of agnosticism seems to implicitly hold that this state of not-knowing is only temporary, that eventually, after we die, all will become evident or clear. Such was Aquinas' understanding of heaven as the disclosure of "Truth" when the individual's soul will see and understand things as God does, that in the words of Psalm 36, "in Thy light we will see light."[6] Either that, or else as in the Buddhist quest for *nirvana*, (literally a "blowing out" — as of a candle's flame) we will be delivered from the self-absorbed agony or distress of not-knowing — as if we each constituted the center of our own universe.

But if these visions of a final enlightenment seem naïve, are they any more so than that of an atheistic scientism which seems to assume that since modern science has largely destroyed most of the more primitive notions of the gods or of almighty God, that, despite what Einstein thought, sooner or

Einstein and the Image of God

later science will eventually solve all the mysteries that still remain? If this isn't a faith of sorts, then what is?

This in turn brings us around the circle again. Einstein did not believe in an afterlife, so the idea that we, as individuals, would become more enlightened after we die would be, for him, entirely ruled out. After all, from this point of view, after we die we shall know nothing — not even be aware that we're dead!

But what about humanity in general: will not future generations eventually know more? In fact, isn't this already the case now, sixty or more years since Einstein's death? Have not the frontiers of science expanded exponentially, especially cosmology, particularly with the advent of artificial intelligence to process the immense amount of new data being acquired almost every day? Yes, surely this is true, but it seems there are limits, not the least of which, as we have already seen, is the speed of light. We now know that the Universe started approximately 13.8 billion years ago, with contemporary deep space imaging techniques detecting faint galaxies apparently formed as far back as about 11 billion years ago — all which leads us to suspect that the Universe may extend even farther out into space. But will the human race ever continue to exist long enough to detect the farthest edge of the Universe — assuming there is one?

The odds make it seem unlikely, even if humanity survives another million years, especially considering the cosmic light speed-limit and that we have only about 300,000 years separating us from the time proto-humans first emerged from the African rainforests. And given established estimation that the Sun will eventually go into a "red giant" phase several billion years from now, frying planet Earth to a crisp if not swallowing it up altogether, leaves us little hope that we'll ever learn much more, cosmologically speaking, than we are

Afterthoughts

able to guess already. This is probably the case, even if we manage to survive a severe warming of the planet before the next scheduled ice age begins, which, if the pattern of the past million years continues, is due about 20 to 30 thousand years from now.

What all this adds up to, I think, at least in terms of my own convictions, is a prediction that something resembling a religious faith will always survive, regardless of the rise and fall of particular formulations of doctrines and institutions. My reasoning this matter is based on psychiatrist Viktor Frankl's observation that humans cannot cope with, or much more, flourish, without a sense of *meaning* or purpose to their lives.[7] Once life becomes meaningless, survival itself becomes question-able. Religion, according to Frankl's brand of existential psychology, can be defined as "the search for ultimate meaning" and faith as "trust in ultimate meaning."[8] Since reading those definitions in the Preface of what was Frankl's first book, but was, in fact, only published in English as his last, I've often wondered: is that trust in any particular understanding of ultimate meaning, or simply a trust that there is one — even if it remains obscure or still unknown?

But in the face of the scientific facts related above, the problem or question today becomes all the more evident: it is the survival, not just of meaning, but of life itself, and that, not just for individuals but for our whole universe, and even that, for how long?

I ask this question in full awareness that during the time I still live (I had grandfather who lasted until age 95), and despite John Horgan's 1996 prediction of *The End of Science*, the shoals of scientific opinion could shift yet again.[9] If that happens, despite having to leave some extra space at the end of the chapters for additional comments or observations, perhaps I will have to produce another edition of this book. But until, or if, that happens, then this edition will, with minor corrections, or perhaps a few additions to these afterthoughts, will have to do. Beyond that, the implications of what the passage of time has in regard to ultimate reality and meaning may have to remain the topic of still another book.

---

[1] 2 Cor 4:4; Col 1:17; Heb 1:3.
[2] For more on Nogar and his last book, see nat.cath.org/NCR_Online/archives2/1998d/120498/120498u.htm
[3] *Teilhard Journal XX (VIII),* 59. The note in French, nevertheless repeats the insistence on "everything — forever" in the Greek words *panta — en es áei,* presumably borrowed from the New Testament.
[4] A microfilmed copy of these same Journals are now available for inspection by scholars at the Woodstock Library at Georgetown University, Washington, DC.
[5] Calaprice, 344.
[6] Psalm 35:10, as occasionally quoted by Aquinas (*ST*, Part I, Q.12, Art.2, Art.5; Part I-II, Q.67, Art.5; *Compendium of Theology*, Chap. 105.
[7] The guiding thesis of Frankl's 1969 best seller, *Man's Search for Meaning.*
[8] Frankl, Viktor. *The Unconscious God,* 1975.
[9] For Horgan's own summary of his book's argument, see www.edge.org/documents/archive/edge15.html (accessed 7-11-15).

Bibliography

The following is a list of books and articles quoted, cited, or consulted in the process of writing this book.

Ali, Irfan. *Three Translations of the Koran Al-Qur'an*. A Public Domain Book (Amazon Kindle edition).

Allegra, Gabriel M., O.F.M. *My Conversations with Teilhard de Chardin on the Primacy of Christ*. Chicago, IL: Franciscan Herald Press, 1971.

Aquinas, Thomas. *Basic Writings of Thomas Aquinas*. New York: Random House, 1945.
_____ *Compendium of Theology*. St. Louis: B. Herder, 1947.

Aslan, Reza. *Zealot: The Life and Times of Jesus of Nazareth*. New York: Random House, 2013.

Augustine. *Collected Works*. Philip Schaff, ed., 1886.

Barrow, John B. *The Origin of the Universe*. New York: Basic Books, 1994.

Barrow, John B. & Tipler, Frank J. *The Anthropic Cosmological Principle*. New York: Oxford University Press, 1988.

Bergson, Henri. Creative Evolution. Trans. By Arthur Mitchell. New York: Henry Holtz, 1911. Public Domain Amazon Kindle Edition.

Birx, H. James 2002 'Nietzsche, Darwin, and Evolution' www.hichumanities.org/Ahproceedings/James%20Birx.pdf (accessed 7/6/11).

Bracken, Joseph A. *The World in the Trinity: Open-Ended Systems in Science and Religion*. Minneapolis, MN: Fortress Press, 2014.

Einstein and the Image of God

Brown, Raymond E. *The Death of the Messiah: A Commentary on the Passion Narratives in the Four Gospels.* New York: Doubleday, 1994.
_____ *The Birth of the Messiah: A Commentary on the Infancy Narrative in the Gospels of Matthew and Luke.* New York: Doubleday, 1998

Brown, Raymond E., Fitzmyer, Joseph A., Murphy, Roland E. *The Jerome Biblical Commentary.* Englewood Cliffs, NJ: Prentice Hall, Inc. 1990.

Catechism of the Catholic Church, 2nd ed., Libreria Editricae Vaticana. English trans. For USA, Washington, DC: United States Catholic Conference, 2000.

Chaisson, Eric J. *Cosmic Evolution: The Rise of Complexity in Nature.* Cambridge MA: Harvard University Press, 2001.

Clark, Ronald W. *Einstein: The Life and Times.* New York & Cleveland, OH: World Publishing, 1971.

Clayton, Philip. *Mind and Emergence: From Quantum to Consciousness.* Oxford, New York: Oxford University Press, 2004.

Cobb, John B. Jr., ed. *Religions in the Making: Whitehead and the Wisdom Traditions of the World.* Eugene OR: Wipf and Stock Publishers, 2012.

Colledge, Edmund & McGinn, Bernard. Transl. *Meister Eckhart:* New York: Paulist Press, 1961.

Collins, William E. *Creation and Science.* London: Catholic Truth Society/Ignatius Press, 2011.

Cooper, John W. *Panentheism: The Other God of the Philosophers.* Grand Rapids, MI: Baker Academic, 2006.

Bibliography

Cousins, Ewert H., ed. *Process Theology: Basic Writings.* New York: Newman Press, 1971.

Cusa, Nicholas of. *Selected Spiritual Writings.* Trans, by H. Lawrence Bond. Mahwah, NJ: Paulist Press, 1997.

Damasio, Antonio. *Looking for Spinoza: Joy, Sorrow, and the Feeling Brain.* New York: Houghton Miflin, 2003.

Darwin, Charles. *The Origin of Species.* New York: Random House, 1979,

Dawkins, Richard *The God Delusion.* New York: Houghton Miflin, 2006, 2008.

DeLubac, Henri. *The Mystery of the Supernatural.* Montreal: Palm Publishers, 1957.

Dennett, Daniel C. *Darwin's Dangerous Idea: Evolution and the Meanings of Life.* New York: Simon & Schuster, 1995.
_____*Breaking the Spell: Religion as a Natural Phenomenon.* New York: Viking, 2006.

Denzinger, Henrico. *Enchiridion Symbolorum.* Freiburg: B. Herder, 1911.

Dworkin, Ronald. *Religion Without God.* Cambridge, MA: Harvard University Press, 2013.

Eagleton, Terry. *Culture and the Death of God.* New York, London: Yale University Press, 2014.

Eliade, Mircea. *The Sacred and the Profane,* 1957.

Einstein and the Image of God

Erhman, Bart D. *How Jesus Became God: The Exaltation of a Jewish Preacher from Galilee.* New York: HarperCollins, 2014.

Farrell, John. *The Day Without Yesterday: Lemaître, Einstein and the Birth of Modern Cosmology.* New York: Thunder's Mouth Press, 2005; New eBook edition, Farrellmedia, Inc., 2012.

Fitzmyer, Joseph A. *Scripture and Christology: A Statement of the Biblical Commission with a Commentary.* New York/Ramsey, NJ: Paulist Press, 1986.

Flew, Anthony with Roy Abraham Varghese. *There is a God: How the World's Most Notorious Atheist Changed His Mind.* New York: HarperCollins, 2007.

Fowler, James W. *Stages of Faith: The Psychology of Human Development and the Quest for Meaning.* New York: Harper & Row, 1981.
_____ *Becoming Adult: Becoming Christian: Adult Development and Christian Faith.* New York: Harper & Row, 1984.

Frankl, Viktor E. *Man's Search for Meaning: Existentialism and Psychotherapy.* New York: Pocket Books, 1959.
_____ *The Unconscious God: Psychotherapy and Theology.* New York: Simon & Schuster, 1975.

Freud, Sigmund. *The Future of an Illusion.* Translated by W.D. Robson-Scott. Mansfield Center, CT: Martino Publishing, 2011.

Froese, Paul & Bader, Christopher. *America's Four Gods: What We Say about God — and What That Says about Us.* New York: Oxford University Press, 2010.

Funk, Robert W., Hoover, Roy W., & The Jesus Seminar *The Five Gospels: The Search for the Authentic Words of Jesus.* New York: Macmillan, 1993.

Bibliography

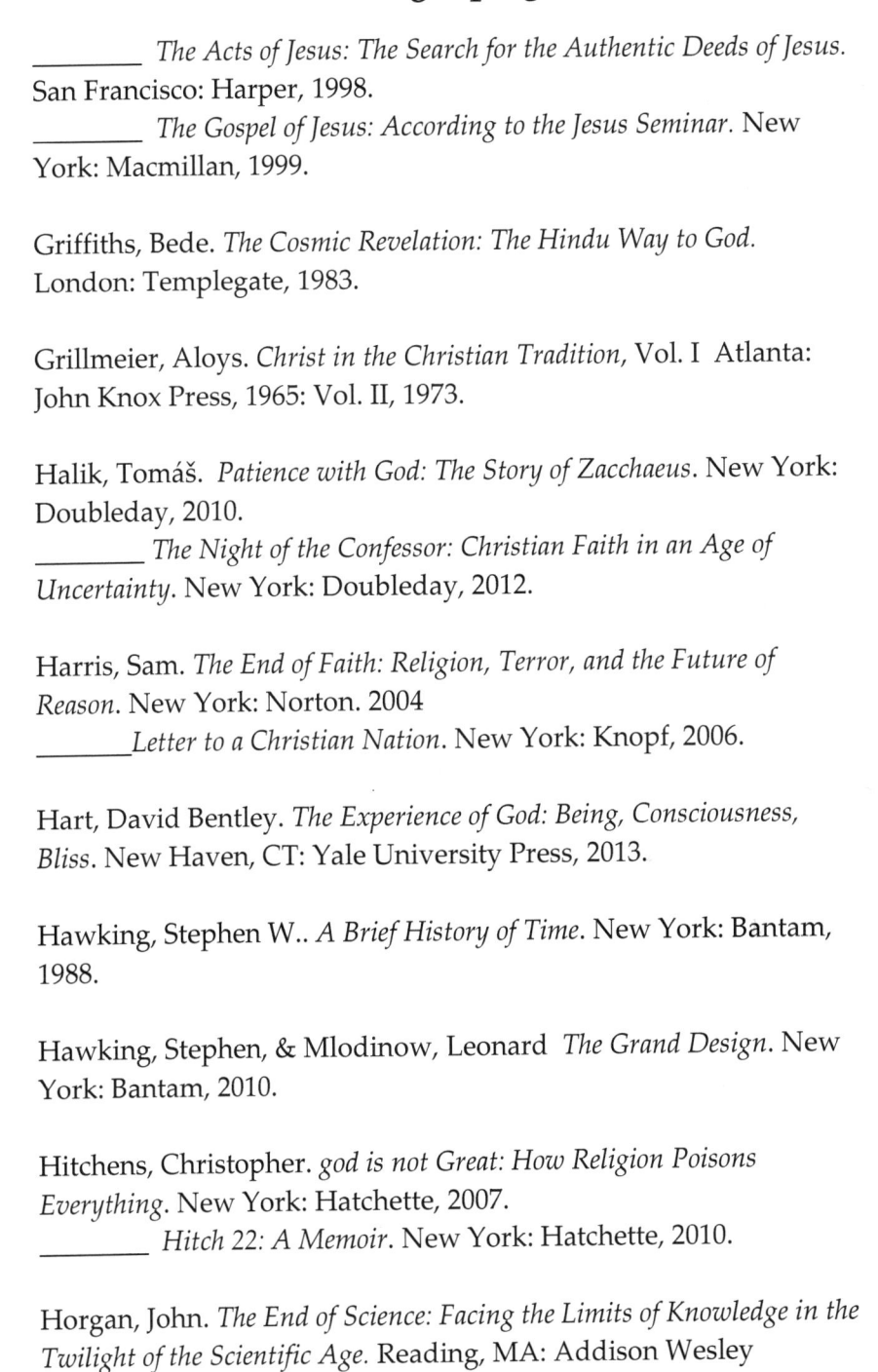

_____ *The Acts of Jesus: The Search for the Authentic Deeds of Jesus.* San Francisco: Harper, 1998.

_____ *The Gospel of Jesus: According to the Jesus Seminar.* New York: Macmillan, 1999.

Griffiths, Bede. *The Cosmic Revelation: The Hindu Way to God.* London: Templegate, 1983.

Grillmeier, Aloys. *Christ in the Christian Tradition*, Vol. I Atlanta: John Knox Press, 1965: Vol. II, 1973.

Halik, Tomáš. *Patience with God: The Story of Zacchaeus.* New York: Doubleday, 2010.

_____ *The Night of the Confessor: Christian Faith in an Age of Uncertainty.* New York: Doubleday, 2012.

Harris, Sam. *The End of Faith: Religion, Terror, and the Future of Reason.* New York: Norton. 2004

_____*Letter to a Christian Nation.* New York: Knopf, 2006.

Hart, David Bentley. *The Experience of God: Being, Consciousness, Bliss.* New Haven, CT: Yale University Press, 2013.

Hawking, Stephen W.. *A Brief History of Time.* New York: Bantam, 1988.

Hawking, Stephen, & Mlodinow, Leonard *The Grand Design.* New York: Bantam, 2010.

Hitchens, Christopher. *god is not Great: How Religion Poisons Everything.* New York: Hatchette, 2007.

_____ *Hitch 22: A Memoir.* New York: Hatchette, 2010.

Horgan, John. *The End of Science: Facing the Limits of Knowledge in the Twilight of the Scientific Age.* Reading, MA: Addison Wesley Publishing, 1996.

Einstein and the Image of God

Isaacson, Walter. *Einstein: His Life and Universe.* New York: Simon & Schuster, 2007.

James, William. *The Varieties of Religious Experience: A Study in Human Nature* (1901), A Public Domain Book (Guttenberg Project edition).

Jammer, Max. *Einstein and Religion.* Princeton, NJ: Princeton University Press, 1999.

John Paul II 'Truth Can Not Contradict Truth'. Address of the Pope to the Pontifical Academy of Sciences, Oct. 22, 1996.

Johnston, William, Ed. *The Cloud of Unknowing and the Book of Privy Counseling.* New York: Doubleday, 1973.

Josephus, Flavius. *The Works of Flavius Josephus.* Translated by William Whiston. Edinburgh: William P. Nimmo, 1865.

Kaufmann, *Walter. Nietzsche: Philosopher, Psychologist, Antichrist.* Princeton, NJ: Princeton University Press, 1974.
_____ *Critique of Religion and Philosophy.* Princeton, NJ: Princeton University Press, 1978.

Kavanaugh, Kieran, and Rodriguez, Otilio, Transl. *The Collected Works of St. John of the Cross.* Washington, D.C.: Institute of Carmelite Studies, 1973.

Kleist, James A., transl. *The Epistles of St. Clement of Rome and St. Ignatius of Antioch.* Westminster, MD: The Newman Press.

Krauss, Lawrence M. *A Universe from Nothing: Why There Is Something Rather than Nothing.* New York: Simon & Schuster, 2012.

Bibliography

Kropf, Richard W. *Teilhard, Scripture, and Revelation: A Study of Teilhard de Chardin's Reinterpretation of Pauline Themes*. Cranbury, NJ: Fairleigh Dickinson University/Associated University Presses, 1980.
Kropf, Richard W. *Evil and Evolution: A Theodicy*. Fairleigh Dickinson/University Associated University Presses, 1984; Eugene, OR: Wipf & Stock, 2004.
_____ *Faith, Security and Risk: The Dynamics of Spiritual Growth*. Mahwah, NJ: Paulist Press, 1990 Eugene, OR: Wipf & Stock Publishers, 2003.
_____ *The Faith of Jesus: The Jesus of History and the Stages of Faith*. Eugene, OR: Wipf & Stock Publishers, 2006.

Lewis, C. S. *The Problem of Pain*. New York: Macmillan, 1962.

Luibheid, Colum, & Rorem, Paul, Transl. *Pseudo-Dionysius: The Complete Works*. New York: Paulist Press, 1987.

Mackie, J. J. 'Evil and Omnipotence', in *Mind*, No. 64, pp. 200-12, 1955.

Maquire, Daniel C. *Christianity without God: Moving beyond the Dogmas and Retrieving the Epic Moral Narrative.*
Albany, NY: State University of New York Press, 2014.

Maritain, Jacques. *The Peasant of the Garonne*. New York: Holt, Rinehart, Winston, 1968.

Mahoney, Jack, *Christianity in Evolution: An Exploration*. Washington, DC: Georgetown University Press, 2011.

McGinn, Bernard, ed. *Meister Eckhart: Teacher and Preacher*. New York: Paulist Press, 1981.

Meier, John P. *A Marginal Jew; Rethinking the Historical Jesus*. New York: Doubleday, 1991, 1994, 2001, 2009.

Metaxas, Eric. "Science Increasingly Makes the Case for God". New York: *Wall Street Journal,* December 26, 2014.

Miller, David L. *The Three Faces of God: Traces of the Trinity in Literature and life.* New Orleans, LA: Spring Journal, Inc., 2005.

Nietzsche, Friedrich W. *Works of Friedrich Nietzsche.* Amazon Kindle Edition.

Nogar, Raymond J. *The Wisdom of Evolution.* New York: Doubleday, 1963.
_____ *The Lord of the Absurd.* New York: Herder & Herder, 1967.

Otto, Rudolph. *The Idea of the Holy.* John W. Harvey, transl., 2nd edition. London: Oxford University Press, 1950.

Panikkar, Raimon. *The Rhythm of Being: The Unbroken Trinity.* Maryknoll, NY: Orbis Books, 2010.

Parini, Jay. *Jesus: The Human Face of God.* Seattle, WA: Lake Union Press. 2013.

Pizzuto, Vincent A. *A Cosmic Leap of Faith: An Authorial, Structural, and Theological Investigation of the Cosmic Christology in Col 1:15-20.* Louven: Peeters, 2006.

Plotinus. *Enneads.* Translated by Stephen MacKenna. London: Penguin Books, 1991.

Polkinghorne, John C. *Chaos, Quarks, and Christianity.* New York: Crossroad/Herder & Herder, 1995.

Quasten, Johannes. *Patrology,* Vols I, II, III. Westminster, MD: Newman Press, 1947.

Bibliography

Rahner, Karl. *The Trinity*. New York: Herder & Herder, 1970.
_____ (ed.) *Encyclopedia of Theology*. New York: Seabury, 1975.

Ratzinger, Josef A. *Co-workers in the Truth*, San Francisco, CA: Ignatius Press, 1992,
_____ *Benedictus: Day by Day with Pope Benedict XVI*. (Peter J. Cameron, ed.) Yonkers, NY: Magnificat-Ignatius Press, 2006.

Reimarus, Hermann S. *Fragments from Reimarus*., Ed. Lessing, G. E., Transl. Voysey, C., London: Williams & Norgate, 1879.

Reiss, Moshe www.moshereiss.org/christianity/04_deadsea/04_deadsea.html (accessed 1/14/2015).

Robinson, John A. T. Honest to God. Westminster: John Knox Press, 1963.

Rubenstein, Richard E. *When Jesus Became God: The Struggle to Define Christianity during the Last Days of Rome*. New York: Houghton, Mifflin, Harcourt, 2000.

Rummel, R. J. *Death by Government: Genocide and Mass Murder*. New Brunswick, NJ: Transaction Publishers,1994. (accessed 7/5/2011).

Sagan, Carl. *Cosmos*. New York: Random House, 1980.

Schweitzer, Albert. *On Finding the Historical Jesus: From Reimarus to Werde*, 1910.
_____ (1914) *The Mystery of the Kingdom of God*. Amherst NY: Prometheus Books, 1985.

Sherburne, Donald W. *A Key to Whitehead's Process and Reality*. New York: Macmillan, 1966.

Einstein and the Image of God

Smith, Wilfred Cantwell. *Faith and Belief.* Princeton, NJ: Princeton University Press, 1979.

Spinoza, Benedict de. *Ethics.* Trans. R.H.M. Elwes. A Public Domain Book, Amazon Kindle edition.

_____ Correspondence. Trans, R.H.M. Elwes www.sacred-texts.com/phi/spinoza/corr/index.htm (accessed 5/12/2015).

Spong, John Shelby. *Christpower: Recovering the Divine at the Heart of the Human.* Richmond VA: Thomas Hale, 1974. Republished in Haworth, NJ: St. Johann Press, 2007.

_____ *Why Christianity Must Change or Die.* New York: HarperCollins, 1998.

_____ *A New Christianity for a New World; Why Traditional Faith Is Dying and How a New Faith Is Being Born.* San Francisco: HarperCollins, 2001.

_____ *Jesus for the Non-Religious.* New York: HarperCollins, 2007.

Steinhardt, Paul, and Turok, Neil. "Endless Universe: Beyond the Big Bang" in *The Universe: leading Scientists Explore the Origin, Mysteries, and Future of the Universe.* New York: Harper Perennial, 2014.

Stenger, Victor J. *The Comprehensible Universe: Where Do the Laws of Physics Come From?* Amherst, NY: Prometheus, 2006.

_____ 'A Scenario for the Natural Origins of Our Universe'. *Philo* 9, No. 2, pp. 93-102, 2006. www.colorado.edu/philosophy/vstenger/Godless/Origins.pdf (accessed 6/30/2011).

_____ *God, the Failed Hypothesis: How Science Shows that God Does Not Exist.* Amherst, NY: Prometheus, 2007.

_____ *Quantum Gods: Creation Chaos, and the Search for Cosmic Consciousness.* Amherst, NY: Prometheus, 2009a.

Stenger, Victor J. *The New Atheism: Taking a Stand for Science and Reason.* Amherst, NY: Prometheus, 2009b.

Bibliography

_____ 'The Grand Accident', www.colorado.edu/philosophy/vstenger/Cosmo/TheGrandAccident.pdf 2010 (accessed June 30, 2011).
_____ *The Fallacy of Fine Tuning: Why the Universe Is Not Designed for Us*. Amherst, NY: Prometheus, 2011.
_____ 'A Case Against Fine-Tuning of the Cosmos' unpublished, see www.colorado.edu/philosophy/vstenger/Fallacy/FTCosmo.pdf (accessed 6/30/2011).

Taylor, Charles. *A Secular Age*. Cambridge, MA: Harvard University Press, 2007.

Teilhard de Chardin, Pierre. *The Phenomenon of Man*. New York: Harper & Row, 1959.
_____ *The Divine Milieu*. New York: Harper & Row, 1960.
_____ *Science and Christ*. New York: Harper & Row, 1965.
_____ *Letters from a Traveler*, New York: Harper and Brothers, 1968.
_____ *Human Energy*. London: Collins, 1969.
_____ *The Activation of Energy*. London: Collins, 1970.
_____ *Christianity and Evolution*. London: Collins, 1971.
_____ *Toward the Future*. New York: Harcourt Brace Jovanovich, 1975.
_____ *The Heart of Matter*. New York: Harcourt Brace Jovanovich, 1978.
_____ *Journals* 8-21, (1944-1955) unpublished.

Vitz, Paul C. *Faith of the Fatherless: The Psychology of Atheism*. 2nd edition, Dallas, TX: Spence Publishing Co, 1999.
_____ *Psychology as Religion: The Cult of Self-Worship*. 2nd edition, Grand Rapids, MI: Wm. B. Eerdmans, 1994.

Wallace, Stanley, ed. *Does God Exist? The Craig-Flew Debate*. UK: Ashgate, 2004.

Einstein and the Image of God

Watson, Kirk, transl. *The Good Atheist: Three Early Biographies of Spinoza* by Bayle, Lucas, and Colerus. Amazon Kindle Books.

Watson, Peter. *The Age of Atheists: How We Have Sought to Live since the Death of God.* New York: Simon & Schuster, 2014.

Weisel, Elie. *Night.* New York: Avon Books, 1972.

Whitehead, Alfred North, & Russell, Bertrand. *Principia Mathematica.* Cambridge, U.K.: Cambridge University Press, 1910, 1913, 1927.

Whitehead, Alfred North. *Religion in the Making.* New York: New American Library, 1974.
_____ *Adventures in Ideas.* New York: Free Press. 1967.
_____ *Process and Reality: An Essay in Cosmology.* Corrected Edition. New York: Free Press, 1978.

Wright, N. Thomas. *The Challenge of Jesus: Rediscovering Who Jesus Was and Is.* Wheaton IL: Intervarsity Press, 1999a.
_____ "Five Gospels but No Gospel: Jesus and the Seminar" in *Authenticating the Activities of Jesus,* ed. Bruce Chilton & Craig A. Evans, Leiden: Brill, pp. 83-120, 1999b.

Index

Adam and Eve, 133
Agnosticism, agnostics, 3-4, 10, 19, 22, 30, 106, 161; Einstein's, 3-4, 161, 174; three forms of, 174
Aim, initial or subjective, 66, 129-30, 154-55
Allegra, Gabriel, 133, 181
Alexandria, school of, 16, 83, 110-13, 117-18, 125; Library of 111
Animism, 68
Angels, Angel Christology, 51, 108-09
Anthropic Principle, 42-43, 44, 181
Antioch, school of, 110-13, 117, 125, 160
Apocalyptic, apocalypticism, 90-91
Apollinaris of Laodicea, 116, 150
Apophaticism, 10, 159-62
Aquinas, Thomas, 15, 28, 133, 159, 161, 171-72, 175, 181
Aristotle, 36, 38-39, 41, 51, 55, 67, 144, 172
Artson, Bradley Shavit, 127-28, 130
Arius, Arianism, 112-13, 115-16
Aseitas, 151
Asimov, Isaac, 44
Aslan, Reza, 95-97, 99, 104, 181
Asperger's Syndrome, 18
Atheism, atheists: 1, 3, 7, 15, 35; and Autism, 18; definition of, 15; growth of, 6; New, ix,-xi, xiii, 6, 8, 26, 40, 51, 71; proof for, 35; psychology of, 17-18
Atonement, concept of, 166
Attestation, multiple, 80
Augustine, St.: desire or longing, 131-32; evolution, 7; God as Being, 38-39, 141, 148, 149, 153, 155; on God and Evil, 46; on God as Person, 28; on Predestination, 153; Works of, 181
Augustus, Caesar, 79
Barnabas, Epistle of, 163
Baron-Cohen, 18
Barrow, John, 42, 44, 181

Einstein and the Image of God

Baylor University study, 19-22, 30, 182
Being, concept of, 39
Belief(s): in general, 50, 164; religious, xi, xv, 1- 2, 27, 30, 33-34, 37, 45, 55, 66, 83, 104-05, 108, 112, 164-69; scientific, 42, 50-51, 160, 163.
Benedict XVI, pope, 35
Berdyaev, Nicolai, 104
Bergson, Henri, 129, 143-44, 181
Bible, Biblical: Commission, Pontifical, 80-83,103, 111, 184; interpretation 7, 69, 80, 86; levels of tradition 80-83, 95-96; scholarship, 1; translations of, xiii, 83, 87, 106, 107, 109, 112, 151
Big Bang, 37-38, 39, 42, 190
Boethius, 28
Bonaventure, St., 7, 160
Bonhöffer, Deitrich, 68
Bracken, Joseph A., 132, 159, 181
Brown, Raymond, 79, 82, 95, 182
Bruno, Giordano, 143
Buddha, Buddhists, 78, 79, 148-49, 161-62, 165, 174
Bultmann, Rudolph, 2, 69
Byzantine, Church & Empire, 121, 160
Calvin, Jean; Calvinism, 62, 167
Catholic Church, xii, 6, 10, 17, 19, 76, 83, 89, 91, 119-20; Biblical Commission of, (see Bible); Doctrinal Commission (Inquisition), 56, 157-58
Chaisson, Eric, 49, 51, 182
Chalcedon, Council of, 118-19, 121, 140, 166; assessment of, 121
Chance, (randomness), 48-50, 129, 140
Christ: cosmic, 9, 131-40, 141, 144, 149, 156, 175; of faith, 1-2, 98, 103-22, 176; as Image of God, 1, 2, 9, 72, 121, 136-38, 144, 150, 156, 162, 166; as Head of the Church,138-39; as "lure", 131-32, 156; as Prophet, Priest, and King, 167-68; Real or Trans-Christ, 142; as Redeemer, 132, 140, 142-43; role in creation, 132, 134, 136, 138-39; as "Suffering Servant", 166; third nature of, 140.
Christianity, Christians, x, xiv, 1, 2, 9, 19, 85, 139; doctrinal dilemma,

Index

122; early growth of, 165; once-born","born again","twice born", 24-25; nominal, 22; "non-theistic", 67-69; "religionless", 68; survival in Middle East, 120,
Christocentric mysticism, 132
Christology: Angel-, 108-09; High, 106-08, 112-113, 132, 154, 156, 162;
    Low, 105, 107, 113, 132, 153, 155; definition of, 148; Spirit-, 113.
Christological Problem, 119-20, 150-56
Church as Body of Christ, 138-39
Clement of Alexandria, 15, 112, 125
Cobb, John A., 146 n.1, 182
Colossians, Epistle to, 9, 103, 105, 113, 136-39, 143, 156, 188
Concurrence, divine, 151-53
Congregation for the Doctrine of the Faith (CDF), 35, 83
Corinthians: First Epistle to, 103, 164; Second Epistle to, 103, 122, 138-39
Constantine, Emperor, 114-15
Constantinople: 114; First Council of, 116; Third Council of, 119
Constantius, Emperor, 116
Consubstantiality, 115, 118
Conversion, religious, 24-25
Copernicus, 56, 126, 136, 165
Coptic Church, 111, 118-19, 121; Catholic-Orthodox dialogue with, 121
Cordovero, Moshe, 127
Cosmic Christ, (see Christ, Cosmic)
Cosmology, xii, 2, 125
Cosmological Argument for God, 34, 42, 44
Cosmological Constant, 37, 43
Craig, William, 39, 52 n13, 193
Creation, concept of, 36
Creeds, xv, 81, 115-16, 137-38, 143
Criteria, exegetical: of Discontinuity, 81; Multiple attestation, 80
Cromwell, Oliver, 56
Crucifixion, 94, 97
Cusa, Nicholas, 162-63, 174, 181

Einstein and the Image of God

Cyril of Alexandria, 117
Cyril of Jerusalem, 116
Damasio, Antonio, xiii, 183
Darwin, Charles, xi, 7, 49, 63, 165, 168, 181, 183
David, King, 82-83, 153
Dawkins, Richard, xi, xiv, 68, 183
Dead Sea Scrolls, 97
Deism, classic 3, 22, 55-57; new, 55
DeLubac, Henri, 152, 183
Demiurge, 113, 150
Dennett, Daniel, xi, 3, 68, 183
Design, Intelligent, 40-44
Determinism, xiv, 5, 45-46, 62, 66, 130
Devil, 85, 120
Divine nature, 60, 115, 118, 126, 140; human share in, 152-54
Divinity, degrees of, 151-52
DNA to RNA conversion, 40
Docetism, 108
Dworkin, Ronald, 3-4, 183
Ebionites, 108
Eckhart, Johann, 157-59, 182, 185
Egypt, flight to, 82; Christianity in, 111, 118-19, 121
Ehrman, Bart, 69, 106-08, 152-55, 184
Einstein, Albert: ix-x, xiv-xv; as agnostic, 3, 4, 177-78; and atheism, 3, 7, 25, 45; autistic?, 18; concept of God 3-8, 17-18, 23-24, 28-29, 31, 35, 41, 50, 70, 72, 104, 122, 126, 129; cosmological constant, 37, 43, 134-35; on free will, 45-46, 49, 130; on Freud, 16-17; meetings with Hubble and Lemaître, 44, 134-35; on gravity waves, 37; on Jesus, 9, 18, 77, 85, 87; and pantheism, 24, 57, 71; on problem of evil, 45-46, 50; on quantum mechanics, 48, 66; on stages of religion, 25-26, 167-68; and Spinoza, xiv-xv, 4-9, 24, 49-51, 61-62, 124
Emotion, Feelings, 15-16
Energy, "dark", 38, 43
Enlightenment, 55-57
Entropy, 37

Index

Ephesians, Epistle to, 103, 105, 107, 137-39, 143
Ephesus, Council of, 117
Epicurus, 46
Erikson, Erik, 25
Eriugena, John Scotus, 59
Ethiopia, Church in, 118, 121
Eusebius, of Caesarea, 89, 113, 167
Eusebius of Nicomedia, 113
Eusebians, (Semi-Arians), 116
Evil, problem of, 45-49, 66, 126, 128, 129, 186
Evolution xv, 8-9, 41, 48-49, 51, 57-63, 64, 126-29, 131-34, 140, 143-44, 150, 155, 168, 174
Exigency, existential, 175
Existence, ix, 36-40, 61, 64, 147, 151-52, 158; categories of, 65; as distinguished from Being, 39, 158: see also "Being", "God", "Ontology"
Exoplanets, 135, 140-41, 156
Faith, xi, xii; and belief, 1, 2, 10, 17, 24-27, 31, 38, 49, 164-70; definitions of, 164; and hope, 163; conjunctive stage, 26; and security needs, 26, 184; stages of, 25-27, 166-69, 184, 187; unitive, 27
Feynman, Richard, 45-46
Flew, Anthony, 38, 40-42, 184
Frankl, Viktor, 25, 179-80, 184
Freedom, (free-will): and chance, 5, 48-49; and Einstein, 45, 62; and Spinoza, 62
Fowler, James W., 25-26, 164, 184
Freud, Sigmund, 16-18, 20, 30, 184
Fundamentalism, 7, 26, 41, 91
Galaxies, number of, 134, 140, 180
Galilee, 82; Roman occupation of, 95-96
Galileo, 56, 126, 136
Gallup Poll, 19-22
Gamow, George, 42-43
Gautama, Siddartha (see Buddha, Buddhism)
Genesis, Book of, 6, 36, 125, 133

Einstein and the Image of God

Geocentrism, 135
Gethsemane, 97
Gnosticism, 92, 120, 137, 147n30
God: definitions of, 3, 15, 28, 47; acts of, 47, 49; as almighty or all-powerful, 15, 47-48; antecedent or primordial nature of, 64, 66; as architect, 22; attributes of, 60-62, 66; as authoritative, 20; as benevolent, 21, 47; as "becoming", 67, 143; as "Being" in itself, xiv, 39, 60, 64-65, 67, 69-70, 143, 153-56, 159-60; "beyond God", 157-61; completion of, 137, 143; consequent nature of, 64, 93, 139; as critical, 21-22; as designer, 40-41, 43; as distant, 22-23, 26; and evil, 45-49; extensions of, 61; as Father, 16-18, 29; as "fellow sufferer", 66, 130, 162; as first cause, 38; "God-head", 157; as good, 46-47; as "ground", 69-70, 157; Incarnation of God, 93, 102, 104-05, 138-39, 141; God of Jesus, 131; and metaphysical principles, 65; modifications of, 62; name of, 88, 106, 111; and nature, xiv, 58-59; as "other" 65; as person, 3, 5, 8, 16, 18, 20, 23, 27-30, 68, 70; personification of, 68, 70, 144, 147; proofs for, 14, 34-35, 50-51, 166, 174; as prime or unmoved mover, 38, 65, 145; as Trinity, 28, 29-30, 68, 156-58, 160-61
Griffiths, Bede, 147, 185
Grillmeier, Aloys, 67, 185
Halik, Tomáš, 27, 185
Harris, Sam, xi, 185
Hartshorne, Charles, 63
Hart, David Bently, 29-30, 35, 185
Hawking, Steven, 43-44
"Heat Death" (see, Universe, future of)
Herschel, William, 134
Hinduism, Hindus, 156, 162, 185
Hitchens, Christopher, x, xiii, 185
Hitler, Adolph, 46, 126
Holocaust, the, 45, 46
Holy Spirit, 29, 113-14, 152, 154, 155
Homoousios (Consubstantiality), 115, 118
Hope, 21, 38, 70, 162-67, 176, 179
Horgan, John, 177, 185

Index

Hosea, Prophet, 6, 83
Hosios of Cordova, 115
Hoyle, Fred, 37
Hubble. Edmund, 36-37, 42, 135, 142, 156
Human nature, xiii, 5, 148-152, 184
Hymns in the New Testament, 106-07, 112, 137-38
Icons, Iconoclasm, 2, 120, 144, 173
Ignatius of Antioch, 110-11, 186
Images of God, 1-2, 9, 18, 20, 21, 30-31, 57, 64-65, 69-70, 120-21, 144-45; Christ as, 1, 136-38, 144-45, 149, 155-60, 162, 166-71, 173; defense of use, 121-22
Immanence, divine, 56, 152
Incarnation: 106; as central to Christianity, 104, 141; development of doctrine of, 105-06; as "innoculation" of the universe, 141; multiple incarnations? 152; reasons for, 133-34, 140, 142
Inquisition, 54, 159
Islam, Muslims, x, xiv, 68, 120; effect on Christianity, 121; growth of, 119-120; idea of God, 68-69; rejection of imagery, 149-50; veneration of Mohammed, 142; view of Jesus, 95
James, William, 24-25, 34; on escapism, 44; on proofs of God, 34; on religious experience, 24-25, 30; on science of religion, 33; on theology, 33; "Will To Believe", 44; works of, 186
Jammer, Max, 186
Jefferson, Thomas, 55, 57, 90
Jerusalem, destruction of, 86, 93-95, 104-05
Jesus, 1, 68-71; birth and infancy, 82-84; death of, 94-98; disciples of, 78, 98; divinity of, 93, 105-22, 153; Einstein on, 9, 77, 86, 122; existence of, 77-79; God of, 131; historic, 79; human nature of, 120, 142, 159; "I am" sayings, 111; as "Image of God" (see Christ as Image); as "Lord", 106-07, 153; miracles of, 84-87; resurrection of, 81, 97-98, 104; second coming of, 90, 93-94, 99, 104; as "Son of God",104, 106, 113, 117, 140, 150, 153, 155-56; as "Son of Man", 97-98, 104, 155; teachings on "Kingdom", 69, 87-94, 99, 105
Jesus Seminar, 67, 85, 92, 96-97, 184, 192

Einstein and the Image of God

John, Apostle, Evangelist: First Epistle of, 31, 108; Gospel of, 83, 88, 96, 98, 105, 107,109, 111; John & Paul compared, 105-110
John the Baptist, 91
John of the Cross, 27, 162
Josephus, 78, 85, 96
Judaism: x, xiv; and evolution, 132; Hasidic, 128-29; and concept of Incarnation, 156; Kabbalist, 128; Second Temple period, 92, 108
Judea, 82, 94-96
Justin Martyr, 99-100,152
Kant, Immanuel, 134
Kaufmann, Walter, ix, 186
Kenosis, 107, 168
Kerygma, 81, 98, 103
Kingdom of God (of Heaven), 65, 69, 87-94, 97, 105
Kohlberg, Lawrence, 27
Krauss, Lawrence, xii-xiii, 37, 43-44, 186
Küng, Hans, 29
Lactantius, 114
Laodicea, 116,137
Life, extraterrestrial, 138-41; origins of, 40, 135
Lee, Bernard, 131
Leibniz, Gottfried Wilhelm, 48
Lemaître, Georges, 37, 42, 134-35, 184
Leo I, Pope (the Great), 118, 168
Lessing, Gotthold,, 90, 99
Lewis, C. S., 47-48, 187
Logos, 83, 112
Luke, Gospel of, 56, 82-83, 88-89, 113-14, 169, 172
M-theory, 44
Maccabbees, Second book of, 36
Mahoney, Jack, 108, 187
Maguire, Daniel, 68, 187
Manichaeism, 120
Mark, Gospel of, 82, 86, 88,-89, 90, 92, 98, 105, 111
Mary Magdalene, 92
Mary, virgin "Mother of God" (*Theotokos*), 19, 82-83, 113-14

Index

Matthew, Gospel of, 82-83, 86, 88-89, 92, 96, 106
Maximus the Confessor, 162
Meier, John P., 78, 80-81, 84-86, 95-96, 99; on "four enigmas", 97-98, 187
Messiah, 79; 82, 90; concept of, 97; double or two Messiahs, 99-100
Miller, David L., 28 n.16, 188
Miracles, 84-86; types of, 84
Mohammed, 95, 120, 148
Monism, xiv, 55
Monogenism, 135
Monophysitism, Monophysites, 118-19, 121, 148, 162
Monotheism, 149, 156
Monothelitism, 119
Moses, 88, 150, 164
Multiverse, 8, 37, 43, 50, 144
Nag Hammadi, 78, 92
Nature, Book of, 7
Nazareth, 82
Nazis, 46
Nephesh, 149
Nero, Emperor, 110
Nestorius, Nestorianism, 116-17, 121
Newton, Isaac; Newtonian Universe, 53, 85, 129
Nicea, First Council of, 2, 114-16; Second, 121
Nicene Creed, 115-16, 117, 143
Nietzsche, Friedrich, ix, 7, 37, 188
Nirvana, 177
Nogar, Raymond, 173-75, 181 n2, 188
Nothing, nothingness, xii-xiii, 37-38, 43
Occam, William of, 87
Old Testament (*Tenach*), 6, 18, 20, 68, 83, 106, 126, 151; anthropology, 151; cosmology, 125; wisdom books, 36, 83, 112, 151, 156
Oldenburg, Henry, 56, 58, 60
Omega, Omega Point, 140, 145, 158
Ontology, xi-xii, 154
Origen of Alexandria, 112-113, 125, 143

Original Sin, 133
Panentheism, 55, 62, 128, 182
Panikkar, Raimon, 30, 156, 188
Pantheism, xiv, 4, 24, 69, 158; two forms of, 55-56
Parmenides, 36
Particularity, scandal of, 142-43
Pascal, Blaise, 131
Paul, 56, 110, 153, 162; Pauline, Epistles, 82, 89-90, 137-39; authentic vs. disputed, 90, 103, 105, 107; identity and role of Jesus in, 110-12, 122, 137-39, 153; on resurrection, 165; on salvation, 167
Paulicianism, 120
Person, concept of, 27
Peter, St., 110-11; Second Epistle of, 153
Pharisees, 109
Philo of Alexandria, 83, 112, 156
Philosophy, ix, xiii-xiv, 1, 5, 30, 33, 44, 55, 61, 189; absolutistic, 44; Greek, 112, 129, 143; Neo-Platonist, 151; of process, 156-58; speculative, 44; Stoic, 83, 112, 125; relationship to theology, 53, 125, 131, 151
Piaget, Jean, 25
Pilate, Pontius, 94-95
Pius X, pope, 92
Pizzuto, Vincent A., 137-38, 188
Plato, Platonism, 36, 53, 62, 116, 123, 152
Pleroma, 139, 141, 164
Plotinus, 62, 128, 188
Polkinghorne, John, 49, 188
Polycarp of Smyrna, 110
Polytheism, 149
Positivism, positivists, 26
Predestination, 155
Prehension, 130-31
Process Philosophy and Theology, 56, 62-65, 69, 156-58, 182
Pseudo-Dionysius, 160-63, 187
Psychē, 151-152
Ptolemy, 125-26

Index

Pythagoreans, 62, 125-26
Q-source in Matthew, Luke, 89
Quantum Mechanics, 48-49, 64, 85, 129-30; Vacuum, xii-xiii, 38, 43, 48-49, 50
Rahner, Karl, 29, 68, 188-91
Randomness, 48-49, 129-30
Ratzinger, Josef (Benedict XVI, Pope), 10, 35
Rationalism, xi, 51, 55, 86
Reason, 3, 10, 16, 23, 33-50, 53, 176; creative, 35; God of, 149-50, 154, 156; priority of, 35, 53
Reconciliation, 8, 122, 132, 138, 142
Redemption, 91, 133, 137, 144
Reformation, 54
Regression, infinite, 39
Reiss, Moshe, 102 n42, 189
Reimarus, Hermann, 89-90, 92, 99-100, 105, 189
Religion, x, xi, xii, 1; conflict with science, 8, 10; cosmic, xv-xvi, 5, 23; Frankl's definition of, 179; future of, 16, 179; organized, 5; origin of, 16, 66; science of, 33; stages or levels of, 25-27, 65-66, 166-69, 187
Renan, Ernest, 91
Resurrection: belief in, 159; of Christ, 57, 81, 90, 95, 165; general, 151, 165; as "meta-historical", 104
Revelation, ix, xv, 7, 55, 149, 185
Revolutions, scientific, etc. 54, 126, 136-37, 170
Robinson, J.A.T., 2, 66, 189
Ruach, 151, 156
Rubenstein, Richard, 67, 189
Rublev, Andrei, 2, 144, 176
Russell, Bertrand, 61
Sacrifice, 6, 169
Sadducees, 96, 109
Schweitzer, Albert, 89-91, 105, 189
Science, x, xii, xv, 10, 33; faith in, 37, 50-51, 163, 178-80; -fiction, 44, 51; limits of, 178, 180, 183; philosophy of, xi, 61; and religion, 132, 176, 179

Einstein and the Image of God

Scientism, 26
Scotus, John Duns, 133-34
Second Coming, 90-91, 99, 104-05
Second Council of Nicea, 121
Second Temple Judaism, 92, 108
Second Vatican Council, 93-94
Severus of Antioch, 162
Sin, original, 133
Smith, Wilfred Cantwell, 166, 189
Socrates, 6, 78
Soul or life-force, xiii-xiv, 27, 66, 88, 112, 116, 128, 151-53, 159
Spinoza, Benedict de (Baruch), xiv, 4, 18, 23-24, 48-50, 53, 190; *Ethics*, 49; and free-will, 45, 50, 60-61; idea of God 8, 23-24, 54, 56-59; "God or Nature", 57-58; Jesus, admiration for, 9; and pantheism, 54, 55; *Tractatus theologico-politicus*, 56
Spong, John Shelby, 29, 66-69, 77, 190
Steinhardt, Paul, 38, 52, 190
Stenger, Victor J., xii-xiii, 55, 65, 190
Stoicism, 110
Substance, concept of, 28, 58
Survival of the fittest, 127
Sylvester, Pope, 113
Tacitus, 95
Teilhard de Chardin, Pierre, xv, 9, 49, 129, 131-37, 139, 141-142, 149, 157-158, 164, 170, 175, 186, 193; contrasted to Whitehead, 143-144, 164; scriptural interpretation, 137-39
Tertullian, 27
Theodicy, 47-48
Theology: definitions, 29
Thomas, Apostle, 109; Gospel of, 92
Tillich, Paul, 29, 68-69, 159
Tipler, Frank, 42, 44
Tradition, levels or stages of, 78-80
Trajan, Emperor, 108
Trinity, Holy, 27-29, 68, 118, 156-58,
Tyrrell, George, 91

Index

Universe(s): age of, 37; cyclical or recurring, 37-38; expansion of, 37, 179; as "flat", 37, 51 n.7, 141; future of, 141-43, 179; multiple, parallel, or "Multiverse", 37, 43, 143-44
Vacuum, quantum, 38, 43
Varghese, Roy A., 40
Vatican Council, First, 84; Second, 93-94
Vitz, Paul C., 17-18, 191
Voltaire, 47-48, 149
Watson, Kirk, 191
Watson, Peter, xiii, 192
Weisel, Elie, 46, 192
Whitehead, Alfred North, xv, 8-9, 57-58, 63-67, 71, 126, 129-130, 132, 139, 192; contrast with Teilhard, 143-44, 157-58, 164
Wisdom, Book of, 36, 151
Wisdom Literature, see Bible, Old Testament
Word (see *Logos*)
Wrede, Georg Wilhelm, 89, 91
Wright, N. T., 67, 93, 192
Xenophanes, 15
Zachariah, Prophecy of, 96
Zealots, 95

Einstein and the Image of God

About the Author

Richard William Kropf, born in Milwaukee, Wisconsin, in 1932, was ordained a priest in 1958 for the Diocese of Lansing, Michigan. He served as parish priest for a number of years, then specialized in philosophical and systematic theology, earning doctorates in theology at the University of Ottawa and the Université St-Paul in Canada. He also has engaged in research both in France and Israel. After a number of years of teaching philosophy, religious studies, theology, and psychology in various Michigan colleges and seminaries, he retired to live a life of prayer and writing in northern Michigan. His published works include the following:

Teilhard, Scripture and Revelation: A Study of Teilhard de Chardin's Reinterpretation of Pauline Themes, published by Fairleigh Dickinson University/Associated University Presses (1980).

Evil & Evolution: A Theodicy, originally published by Fairleigh Dickinson University/AUP (1984): 2nd revised edition published by Wipf & Stock Publishers (2004)

Faith: Security & Risk: The Dynamics of Spiritual Growth, published by Paulist Press in 1990 (republished by Wipf & Stock, 2003).

The Faith of Jesus: The Jesus of History and the Stages of Faith, published by Wipf and Stock Publishers in 2006.

(with Joseph P. Provenzano) *Logical Faith: Introducing a Scientific View of Spirituality and Religion,* published by iUniverse, Inc. (2007, 2009).

Views from a Hermitage: Reflections on Religion in Today's World, published by Lexington Books, Rowman & Littlefield Publishing Group, in 2008.

Breaking Open the Creeds: What Can They Mean for Christians Today?, published by Paulist Press in 2010.

Forever: Evolution and the Quest for Life beyond Life, published by Stellamar Publications, 2012.

Made in the USA
Charleston, SC
03 July 2016